TEACHINGS OF SUFISM

Teachings of

SUFISM

Selected and translated by

CARL W. ERNST, *Ph.D.*

SHAMBHALA
Boston & London
1999

SHAMBHALA PUBLICATIONS, INC.
Horticultural Hall
300 Massachusetts Avenue
Boston, Massachusetts 02115
www.shambhala.com

Printed in The United States of America

⊗ This edition is printed on acid-free paper that meets the
American National Standards Institute Z39.48 Standard.
♻ Shambhala Publications makes every effort to print on
recycled paper. For more information please visit
www.shambhala.com.
Distributed in the United States by Random House, Inc.,
and in Canada by Random House of Canada Ltd

Library of Congress Cataloging-in-Publication Data

Teachings of Sufism/selected and translated by
Carl W. Ernst—1st ed.
p.   cm.
Includes bibliographical references and index.
ISBN 978-1-57062-349-3 (alk. paper)
1. Sufism—Doctrines.   I. Ernst, Carl W., 1950–   .
BP189.3.T38   1999   99–25982
297.4′1—dc21   CIP

CONTENTS

PREFACE

S UFISM HAS BEEN DESCRIBED as the mystical tradition of Islam. That is at best an outsider's description. From the insider's point of view it has been called many different things. "Sufism means that God makes you die to yourself and makes you live in him." "Sufism is a state in which the conditions of humanity disappear." "Sufism is a blazing lightning bolt."

Today Sufism is in fact a contested subject. Its origins lie undeniably in the Islamic religious tradition, and the Qur'an and the Prophet Muhammad have played extraordinarily important roles in Sufism. Although most Muslim societies over the past thousand years have been strongly permeated with the ethical and spiritual perspectives of Sufism, aspects of Sufism have been strongly criticized by reformist and fundamentalist Muslim thinkers in recent years. Foreign scholars hostile to Islam have seen Sufism as an essentially non-Islamic borrowing, and some modern Sufi teachers have presented Sufism as a universal teaching detached from Islam. This debate, by its very nature, cannot be solved from a neutral point of view.

But there has been an extraordinary rise of interest in Sufism in America and Europe in recent years. The Persian poetry of Rumi has attained an unprecedented popularity through the translations of Coleman Barks and others, and the *qawwali* music of Nusrat Fateh 'Ali Khan has become a phenomenon on the world music charts. Surprisingly, aside from some of the poetry of Rumi, not very much of the vast literature of Sufism is easily available in English translations. This book provides a small sampling of Sufi texts on some of the basic aspects of this spiritual path. With perhaps only one exception, none of these writings has appeared in English translation before. In several cases where a French or German translation exists, I have consulted those versions while preparing the English rendition.

Writings on Islamic spirituality and mysticism began to appear in Arabic over a thousand years ago. Since that time, Islam and the Sufi tradition have spread from the Middle East to large parts of Africa, Europe, and much of Asia. In all these places, Arabic has continued to play a leading role in the articulation of Sufism, particularly in relation to the study of the Qur'an and the Islamic religious sciences. After Arabic, Persian was the most widely used language for the expression of religious insight in Muslim countries, and Sufi texts in Persian have been studied in regions as far apart as the Balkans, Egypt, China, and Indonesia. Subsequent elaborations of Sufism have been expressed in many other languages, such as Turkish, Hausa, Urdu, Bengali, and Malaysian. It is far beyond the scope of this book, and certainly beyond my abilities, to represent this enormous literature in its entirety. All the texts translated here are from Arabic and Persian, except for one Urdu selection.

The selection of texts for this anthology has been a matter of personal choice, and so I have selected writings that seemed to me to illustrate well certain aspects of Sufism. In a couple of cases, I have taken more than one text from the same author (Sarraj, Ruzbihan Baqli) because I have personally found them quite attractive. I have chosen texts from widely diverse historical periods, ranging from the tenth century to the twentieth, mostly deriving from the Middle East and India. Brief introductory remarks precede each translation and attempt to place it in a historical and religious context. This collection is basically a companion to my book *The Shambhala Guide to Sufism*, supplementing without repeating any of the texts quoted there. Those who are interested in further details and additional reading suggestions on Sufism can refer to that book, which also lays out the basic approach to Sufism that underlies my translations. A very different and much more wide-ranging survey of Sufi texts and practice will be featured in a volume of translations now in preparation, *Islamic Mysticism: In Practice* (forthcoming from Princeton University Press), which I am editing with contributions from a number of other scholars.

The topics represented here are by no means an inclusive summary, but they are intended to be of interest to those who have become attracted to Sufi teachings today. Since poetry is already the most commonly available form of Sufi literature, I have not attempted to include poetry except when it occurs as part of a Sufi text (there are in fact quite a few verses in both Arabic and Persian quoted throughout this book). Although a couple of selections do have challenging accounts of mystical psychology (the meditation treatises of the Shattari master 'Isa Jund Allah, and some of the passages in Ruzbihan's writings), by and large I have also avoided the more difficult philosophical mystical texts, which to a certain extent are also available in academic writings on Sufism. What this anthology offers, however, is a fairly typical range of teachings as they were communicated from masters to disciples during the past eras of Sufism.

Contemporary readers will be struck by the extent to which the Qur'an forms the backbone of mystical literacy for Sufis, as well as by the frequency with which authors of Persian texts used quotations in Arabic. Numerous long passages and even short code words derived from the Qur'an are sprinkled throughout these pages (with citations preceded by a *Q*), providing a characteristic flavor of Islamic spirituality. In addition to a selection from Sarraj's manual of Sufism devoted to the mystical interpretation of the Qur'an, I have provided an index of Qur'anic passages for the entire book. Readers who compare the Qur'an interpretations of the Sufis with standard translations will be surprised by the range and depth of their mystical exegesis. The spiritual importance of the Prophet Muhammad for Sufis is brought out in two selections: a poetic meditation by the martyr Hallaj and a reverent evocation of the Prophet's character by Sarraj. The spiritual practices of Sufism are represented by selections of several different types: a list of the conditions of discipleship according to Najm al-Din Kubra, several short meditation treatises of the Shattari Sufi order (including some unusual calligraphic representations of the human face), and brief accounts of the practices of several orders by the late North African writer al-Sanusi.

Sufi teachings on mystical love, one of the characteristic

and highly important aspects of this tradition, are represented by a selection from Ruzbihan Baqli's *The Jasmine of the Lovers*, beginning with a dialogue in which an unnamed woman challenges Ruzbihan to define the relationship between human and divine love. This is followed by two short selections on the practice of listening to music; the first, by Ruzbihan, is a highly charged meditation on the spiritual experiences that should occur while listening to music, while the second is from a modern handbook for Sufi singers in India and Pakistan that outlines their ideal behavior. The ethical teachings of Sufism are represented by a short work by Ruzbihan on *The Errors of Wayfarers*, dealing with the subtle deception of the ego known as "infidelity," the nature of love and spiritual companionship, and the master-disciple relationship. This text also contains a fascinating and detailed discussion of the many ways in which one can go astray on the spiritual path.

The master-disciple relationship is further explored in two more texts. One is the testament that the great early master Qushayri appended to his comprehensive treatise on Sufism; he advised disciples to emphasize practices that diminish the ego, including performing service to others, but he also warned disciples not to imagine that masters are immune from sin. This is complemented by a discussion of sainthood from the Central Asian master Simnani, in which he describes the different levels of spiritual experience that saints attain, including the common delusion that one has attained the ultimate goal while in fact one is far away from it.

The final selections are from Sufi biographical literature,

beginning with an account of the great mystical poet Rumi, written a couple of centuries after his death. In addition, there are biographical notices of a number of Sufi women, ranging from ascetics to scholars, coming from ordinary families and from royal dynasties. Since the voices of women typically have not had public prominence in Muslim societies, it is perhaps fitting that they should be given the last word in a book that tries to open Islamic spirituality to a wider audience.

Translation is a difficult task, and it always remains frustrating to some extent. Even if a translator feels confident that the original meaning has been grasped, the first draft of a translation often sticks so closely to the original word order and syntax that it is scarcely comprehensible to the average reader of English. References, code words, quotations, and even the subject of the sentence may not be fully stated. The translator is often faced with a choice between providing detailed footnotes or else producing a kind of expansive translation, which silently inserts an unstated context that the original author thought obvious. In the hope of making these translations user-friendly, I have taken the second course, and I have also dropped the transliteration marks that scholars use to represent the Arabic script. Because the translations are made from Arabic, Persian, and Urdu, there is some variation in the form of personal names, depending on whether the Arabic definite article *al* is used or not (e.g., Sarraj versus al-Sarraj). Although these are not literal, word-for-word translations, I hope that they will prove accessible and generally reliable for those who are interested in how Sufi teachings have been expressed in the past.

In one sense, however, I have retained a feature of these writings (one commonly omitted in most academic translations) that may at first prove challenging to some readers. One must keep in mind that the masters and disciples who used these writings had a profound and emotional reverence for God, the Prophet Muhammad, and all the Sufi saints. They typically expressed this in writing by inserting appropriate formulas of blessing every time the name of any holy person was mentioned. Thus after the name of God, an expression meaning "Most High" typically follows, and the name of the Prophet Muhammad is often followed by the formula "May God bless him and grant him peace." A deceased saint is blessed with the saying "May God sanctify his secret" or "May God be pleased with him." Although at first this may appear strange and cumbersome, if the reader keeps in mind that these sayings are a form of prayer, it may help create some of the mood of devotion that originally accompanied the reading of these texts.

Finally, there remains the pleasant duty of thanking those who have helped bring this particular project about. First of all, thanks to Shambhala editor Kendra Crossen Burroughs, who first suggested the idea for this book. I also appreciate the many positive and encouraging comments from readers of *The Shambhala Guide to Sufism.* I am especially grateful, as always, to my wife, Judith Ernst, for her careful reading of the first draft and for her detailed advice on how to turn it into actual English. The illustrations to the "Meditations of the Shattari Order" are reproduced by the kind permission of the Maulana Azad Library, Aligarh Muslim University, India. Thanks to the University of North Carolina at Chapel Hill for providing me with a much-needed semester of research leave. And let me record here my appreciation for my colleagues (both professors and graduate students) in the North Carolina Triangle universities, who make this such a delightful place to live and work.

I hope this small selection of early Sufi writings provides helpful insights to the growing audience interested in Sufism, both as a historic tradition and as a resource for today.

1

Mystical Understanding of the Qur'an

T HE QUR'AN, the sacred scripture of Islam, is unquestionably of central importance to any understanding
of Sufism. Countless commentaries have been devoted to
bringing out the inner meaning of the Word of God. Some
explanation was indeed necessary, both because of the am-
biguous symbolism found in certain passages and because
of the prominent and enigmatic letters of the alphabet
(such as *TS* and *ALM*) that preface a number of the books
of the Qur'an. A glance at the "Index of Qur'anic Passages
and Prophetic Sayings" at the end of this book will reveal
how extensively quotations from the Qur'an are worked into
the fabric of Sufi thought. Typically, new insights are gener-
ated by juxtaposing verses that contain similar terms. The
following selection is taken from one of the earliest handbooks of Sufi teachings, *The Book of Flashes* by Abu Nasr
al-Sarraj (d. 988). Written in tenth-century Iran during the
period when Sufism was being consolidated as a coherent
body of spiritual teachings, this book gave a comprehensive
picture of how the mystical path was in harmony with all
aspects of Islamic religious law and doctrine. In this selec-

tion, Sarraj insists upon a multilevel interpretation of the sacred text, which corresponds to the different levels of understanding of listeners. This notion of degrees of knowledge and nearness to God is one of the fundamental characteristics of the mystical teachings of Sufism.

The Book of the Elect
On Understanding and Following the Book of God
ABU NASR AL-SARRAJ

On Agreement with the Book of God Most High

The sacred character of the Qur'an. God (who is great and mighty) said, "God is the One who revealed to you the Book; some of its verses have a clearly fixed meaning, and others are symbolic" (Q 3:7). God said, "We brought down from the Qur'an a remedy and a mercy for the faithful" (Q 17:82). God said, "YS! By the wise Qur'an!" (Q 36:1–2). God said, "It is a deep wisdom" (Q 54:5).

The knowledge of the Qur'an. The Prophet said, "The wonders of the Qur'an, the firm rope of God, are endless, nor is it worn out from frequent repetition. One who speaks by it speaks truly, one who acts by it is guided, one who judges by it is just, and one who holds to it is led rightly." It is related by 'Abd Allah ibn Mas'ud (may God be pleased with him) that the Prophet said, "One who seeks knowledge should investigate the Qur'an, for in it is the knowledge of the ancients and the moderns."

Guidance in the Qur'an. God Most High also said, "*ALM!* That is the book not to be doubted. There is guidance in it for those who have faith in the hidden" (Q 2:1–3). The learned know by this remark that there is guidance and explanation for them in the Book of God, which descended upon the Messenger of God (may God bless him and grant him peace). This is the Qur'an; none of the faithful have any doubt that it is from God. This explanation applies to all their difficulties in religious matters after they had faith in the hidden, which means confessing the truth of what God has told them regarding what is hidden from their eyes. Then God said in another verse, "We revealed the Book to you as a clarification for everything, and as a guidance, a mercy, and good news for all those who have submitted" (Q 16:89). This verse teaches the most discerning ones among the learned, after they also had faith in the hidden, that beneath every letter from the Book of God Most High, there is a treasure of understanding reserved for those who are worthy of it, to the extent allotted to them. They conclude this from verses of the Qur'an, such as His saying (He is great and mighty) "We left nothing out of the Book" (Q 6:38), and His saying "We have reckoned up everything in a clear record" (Q 36:12), and His saying "We possess the treasuries of everything, and We do not bring it down except in a known quantity" (Q 15:21). Regarding the meaning of His saying "of everything," they say that it means everything of the knowledge of religion, the knowledge of the spiritual states that occur between humanity and God Most High, and the like.

Only the sound heart understands the Qur'an. In another verse, God (who is great and mighty) says, "The Qur'an guides to that which is most correct" (Q 17:9), that is, it leads to that which is best. The most discerning among the learned know that there is no way to be connected to the best, toward which the Qur'an guides, except by reflection, thought, wakefulness, recollection, and the presence of the heart while reciting it. They also know this from God's saying "It is a Book, which We revealed to you, blessed so they may reflect on its verses, and so those who possess the inner heart may recollect" (Q 38:29). Then the most discerning also realized from this verse that reflection, thought, and recollection cannot be reached except through the presence of the heart. This is because of the saying of God (who is great and mighty), "Truly in that is a remembrance for one who has a heart, or who listens as he witnesses" (Q 50:37), which means presence of the heart. Then one keeps that meaning in mind until the heart recalls another verse where God mentions "a day when wealth and sons do not suffice, except for one who comes to God with a sound heart" (Q 26:88–89). Then he keeps that meaning in mind until God stands in the sound heart as the prayer leader for creation. God (who is great and mighty) said, "Abraham was of God's party, when he came to his Lord with a sound heart" (Q 37:83–84). The most discerning say that in the sound heart there is nothing other than God (who is great and mighty).

The vast meanings of the Qur'an. Sahl ibn 'Abd Allah al-

Tustari said, "If the devotee were given a thousand understandings for every letter of the Qur'an, he would not reach the end of the understanding that God Most High has placed in a single verse of His Book. This is the Word of God Most High, and His Word is His attribute." Just as God has no end, likewise there is no end to the understanding of His Word. The saints understand only to the degree that God Most High has opened their hearts to the understanding of His Word. The Word of God is uncreated, and the intellects of creatures do not reach the end of understanding it, because they are temporal and created. God Most High has mentioned guidance in the Qur'an, calling it "a guidance for those who fear God" (Q 2:2).

On the Special Nature of the Call and the Character of Selection

The selection of the saints. Sahl ibn'Abd Allah said (God have mercy on him), "The call is general but guidance is exceptional." He referred to the saying of the Most High, "God calls to the abode of peace, and He guides whom He wills to the right path" (Q 10:25). For the call is general, but guidance is exceptional, according to relative excellence. This is because God merely turns the will toward himself through the process of guidance. But those whom He chooses, whom He loves, and whom He selects are nearer to Him than those whom He calls. God Most High has also mentioned selection in various places in His Book; in one place: "Say praise to God, and peace upon His servants whom He has selected. Is God better, or that which you

associate with Him?" (Q 27:59). And He refers to peace
for servants whom He has selected and chosen, without
indicating who they are or of what sort they are. Then,
keeping that verse in mind, recall that God said in another
verse, "He selects messengers among the angels and among
humans" (Q 22:75). Some commentators say that "humans"
here means only the prophets. If the previous verse is left
out, one would have to say that selection is only possible
for the prophets. But God also said, "Then We bequeathed
the Book to those of Our servants whom We selected.
Some of them injure themselves, some are in between, and
some excel in good deeds" (Q 53:32). There is a difference
between the selection that He mentions for the messengers
(peace be upon them) and the selection that He mentions
for His servants to whom He bequeathed the Book, for they
are the believers. In the same verse, God explained that
they also differ in the spiritual states that exist between
them and God Most High: "some of them injure themselves," and so on. Selection occurs in two fashions. One
is the selection of the prophets (peace be upon them) for
sinlessness, divine assistance, revelation, and spreading the
message. For the rest of the faithful there is selection for
pure deeds, virtuous struggle, and connection to spiritual
realities and stations.

The goods that God commands. Then God Most High
said, "For each of them We have set a path and a way"
(Q 5:48). And He said, "If God wished, He would have
made you a single community, but He wanted to test you
regarding what has been revealed to you, so vie in doing
good" (Q 5:48). Thus God Most High commended them to

excel, to hasten, and to make effort for good deeds generally. He did not explain what kind of good He told them to
excel in. Then He distinguished and explained this in many
places, like His saying "a guidance for those who fear God"
(Q 2:2); "an exhortation for those who fear God" (Q 2:66);
"fear Me" (Q 2:41); "be in awe of Me" (Q 2:40); "do not fear
them, but fear Me" (Q 3:175); "do not be fearful of them,
be fearful of Me" (Q 2:150); "remember Me, and I will remember you" (Q 2:152); "trust in God" (Q 5:23); "obey God
and obey the Messenger" (Q 5:92); "those who struggle for
Us" (Q 29:69); "whoever gives thanks does so for the good
of his soul" (Q 27:40); "God loves those who are patient"
(Q 3:146); "you were only commanded to worship God, purifying your religion for Him" (Q 98:5); and He also mentioned "men who are truthful about what they have pledged
to God" (Q 33:23).

Detachment from this world. Then He mentioned "the
humble men and women, the sincere men and women, the
patient men and women, and the submissive men and
women" (Q 33:35). In several verses of the Qur'an, He mentions repentance, penitence, resignation, satisfaction, submission, contentment, and giving up wilfulness. Then He
said, "The enjoyment of this world is little, but the next
world is better for those who fear God" (Q 4:77). He said,
"That is the enjoyment of the life of this world, but the best
return is to God" (Q 3:14). "The life of this world is nothing
but play and sport" (Q 6:32). "The life of this world is nothing but deceptive enjoyment" (Q 3:185). Then He said, "We
shall increase the harvest of those who desire the harvest
of the next world, and as for those who desire the harvest

of this world, We shall provide it to them, but they will have no part of the next world" (Q 42:20).

Renouncing desire. Then God mentioned Satan, saying, "Satan is an enemy to you, so take him as an enemy" (Q 35:6). He said, "Have you seen the one who takes his desire as his god? God deliberately leads him astray, seals his hearing and his heart, and places a blindfold over his sight" (Q 45:23). He said, "As for one who rebels, and chooses the life of this world, Hell will be his abode; but as for one who fears the place of his Lord, and denies the desire of the carnal soul, paradise will be his abode" (Q 79:37–41). Many similar things are in the verses by which God Most High has directed humanity toward effort and seeking excellence, toward connection with spiritual realities and taking on their characteristics, and toward truthfulness and sincerity. The faithful are similar insofar as they are receiving that injunction, but they differ in their standing and in their engagement with its realities. All of the faithful are addressed, and they are divided into three levels.

The Differences among Those Who Hear the Speech of God Most High, and Their Levels in Receiving That Speech

The first level: those who love this world. There are those among them who hear, accept, and affirm the speech of God, and they concentrate on these clear verses that are heard, which we have mentioned, as well as on similar ones that we have not mentioned. Between them and the practice of these injunctions, and the enjoyment of the reward that God Most High has promised them, stand barriers: their preoccupation with this world, their heedlessness, their following the carnal soul, their choosing pleasures over duties, their responding to enemies' demands, and their inclination toward the promptings of lust and desires. These are the ones whom God Most High has described in His Book, and He chastised and rebuked them when He said, "Have you seen the one who takes his desire as his god? God deliberately leads him astray" (Q 45:23). God said, "Do not obey one whose heart We have made forgetful of Our remembrance, and who follows his desire" (Q 18:28). He said, "Hold to forgiveness, and order what is right" (Q 7:199). God said, "The people find attractive the love of desires for women and sons. . . . That is the enjoyment of the life of this world, but the best return is to God" (Q 3:14). Then God said (He is great and mighty), "Shall I give you news of something better than that? For those who are devoted, their Lord has gardens with rivers flowing beneath them; they are there eternally, with pure wives, and contentment from God. God oversees His servants" (Q 3:15).

The second level: those who listen to God. There are those among them who hear the speech of God and who answer, repent, are penitent, obey commands, experience spiritual states and abodes, are sincere in practice, and are truthful in their spiritual stations. They are the ones whom God Most High has mentioned in His Book, describing what He has made ready for them. "Those who perform ritual prayer, and who give alms, they are certain of the next world, and they have guidance from their Lord" (Q 31:4–5). God said,

"Those who have faith and act virtuously will have gardens of paradise as their abodes" (Q 18:107). God said, "Whoever acts virtuously, whether male or female, is a believer, and We shall give them a good life and reward" (Q 16:97). Commentators say that "good life" is satisfaction and contentment with God (who is great and mighty). Then God said, "Happy are the believers," and then He describes them as those "who are humble in their prayers, and who shun idle talk . . ." (Q 23:1–3). 'Amr al-Makki said (God have mercy on him), "Everything other than God that occurs in hearts is idle talk." Thus God proclaims that those who affirm God's unity shun everything except God. Then He said, "Those are the heirs who inherit Paradise, where they will be forever" (Q 23:10–11). They are mentioned frequently in the Qur'an. God has distinguished them over others by His mention of them and by His promise to them of a rich reward.

The third level: those who know. The third group of those who are addressed by God are those whom God Most High mentions, whom He honors by relating them to knowledge and awe. God said, "Only the knowers among God's servants are in awe of Him" (Q 35:28). God said, "Those who have knowledge attest that God rules by justice" (Q 3:18). God said "Are those who know equal to those who do not know?" (Q 39:9). He specially chose a group among them, calling them "those who are firmly rooted in knowledge" (Q 3:7), thus adding another meaning to the description by which He honored them. Abu Bakr al-Wasiti said (God have mercy on him), " 'Those who are firmly rooted in knowledge' are those who are rooted by their spirits in the hidden of the hidden, and in the secret of the secret. God gives them much knowledge, and He intends for them the implications of the verses of the Qur'an, which He intends for no one else. They dive into the ocean of knowledge with understanding, seeking yet more. Reserved hidden treasuries of understanding and marvelous texts are unveiled to them beneath every letter and word. They bring out pearls and jewels, and they speak with wisdom."

The knowledge of the saint. There is one among them to whom oceans are but a drop of spit compared with the prerogatives he has witnessed, namely the prerogatives of the knowledge that God Most High has reserved for His prophets and by which He has singled out His saints and pure ones. Such a one plunges into the oceans of understanding with his conscience, with his pure recollection and the presence of his heart, and he finds the precious jewel. He is the one who knows the origins from which the word derives, and he encounters their source. He thus frees others from the need for discussion, study, and investigation. This is a commentary on the saying of al-Wasiti, as was mentioned, and an explanation of what al-Wasiti said is also found in a saying by Abu Sa'id al-Kharraz on the same subject. Abu Sa'id said (God have mercy on him), "The first understanding of the Book of God (who is great and mighty) is its practice, because it contains knowledge, understanding, and interpretation." The first understanding is listening and witnessing, because of the saying of God (who is great and mighty), "In that is a reminder for those who have a heart or give ear and act as witness." (Q 50:37). The Most High also said, "Those who listen to the Word follow the best of it" (Q 39:18). All of the Qur'an is good, but following the best means the wonders unveiled to hearts while hearing and listening by the path of understanding and interpretation.

On Interpreting the Qur'an by Listening and Reflective Presence during Its Recitation, and on Understanding the Divine Speech by How the Worshiper Is Spoken To

Three levels of listening to God. Know that listening and presence while hearing are of three kinds. According to what was transmitted to me, Abu Sa'id al-Kharraz said (God have mercy on him), "The first kind of listening is to hear the Qur'an as though the Prophet (may God bless him and grant him peace) is reciting it to you. Then you go beyond that, and it is as though you hear it from Gabriel (peace be upon him). You hear his recitation to the Prophet (may God bless him and grant him peace), as in the saying of God (who is great and mighty) 'It is the revelation of the Lord of creation, with which the faithful spirit Gabriel descended upon your heart' (Q 26:192–94). Then you go beyond that, and it is as though you hear it from God, as in the saying of God (who is great and mighty) 'We brought down from the Qur'an a remedy and a mercy for the faithful' (Q 17:82), and His saying 'The revelation of the Book is from God the glorious, the wise' (Q 39:1). It is as though you hear it from God Most High, and similarly: '*HM*! the revelation of the Book is from God the glorious, the knowing' (Q 40:1)."

Presence of the heart. The source of understanding is when you listen to God Most High while present in your heart and absent from worldly preoccupations and from your carnal soul. This is done by power of witnessing, purity of recollection, gathering of concentration, good manners, and purity of conscience. Sincere realization and the power of witnessing are the supports that confirm the truth, and the departure from constriction to freedom. Present witnessing is for the penetration of the hidden realm by the hidden realm. Speedy union with the recollected One in the hidden realm is by the word of God, "the gracious and knowing One" (Q 6:103).

Believing in the hidden. The explanation of all this is understood and interpreted from the saying of the Most High, "Those who believe in the hidden" (Q 2:3). Abu Sa'id ibn al-A'rabi said, "They are hidden in God's hiddenness, and through the hidden they believe in the hidden. Even though He is hidden, they do not encounter doubt or deception about Him." The Most High said, "Say, God guides to the truth. Is the one who guides to the truth more worthy to be followed, or one who does not guide except if he is guided?" (Q 10:35). And He said, "What is there other than the truth, except error? You are indeed turning away" (Q 10:32). Abu Sa'id al-Kharraz said (God have mercy on him), "People only comprehend God as the hidden, outside the qualities of realities. That is the same as God's saying 'Those who believe in the hidden' (Q 2:3)."

God is the hidden. The hidden is the affirmation that God Most High makes hearts bear witness to: God's attributes, His names, His self-descriptions, and what the

Scripture tells them. So they affirm the attributes, and they do not pretend to comprehend them totally. Have you not heard the saying of the Most High? "If all the trees in the world were pens, and the ocean, after its creation, helped by seven seas, were ink, the words of God would not be exhausted" (Q 31:27). If the description of his word is not comprehended, and the understanding of it cannot be totally attained, how can the reality of His description, His selfhood, and His essence be comprehended? Therefore, regardless of how the realizers of truth, the ecstatics, the knowers of God, and the affirmers of divine unity refer to him, or how they express Him, or how their expression fails to contain Him, or how their proof does not demonstrate him, or how their allusion does not indicate Him—because of their conflicting knowledge, and the disparity of their spiritual states, stations, locations, and the other things that they have witnessed externally and internally—it is established among the most discerning of the learned that He is indeed the hidden. God Most High described this by His saying "Those who believe in the hidden" (Q 2:3).

2

THE CHARACTER OF THE PROPHET MUHAMMAD

J UST AS THE Holy Book of the Qur'an forms the primary
revelation of God to humanity, so too for Sufis the
Prophet Muhammad serves as the chief example of how a
human being can approach the presence of God. Since the
other prophetic traditions, Judaism and Christianity, did
not have any means of recognizing the authority of Muhammad without compromising their own views, it has been
extremely difficult for outsiders to understand the profound
reverence with which Muslims regard the Prophet. Nevertheless, it must be realized that devotion to the Prophet is
one of the most distinctive and powerful aspects of the Islamic tradition, particularly in Sufism. The two following
selections are both from the early period of Sufism.

THE PROPHET MUHAMMAD
AS PRIMORDIAL LIGHT

THE FIRST PASSAGE is a prose writing from the Sufi martyr
al-Husayn ibn Mansur al-Hallaj. Hallaj is best known in

popular lore for his outrageous pronouncements, such as "I am the Truth," and for his dramatic execution in Baghdad in 922 following a series of drawn-out heresy trials. Yet in this piece he exhibits a tremendous reverence for the Prophet, extolling him with profoundly poetic images that emphasize the cosmic role of the Prophet as the supreme example of spiritual attainment. This is one of ten short writings by Hallaj that were known collectively as *The Book of the* TS's (*Kitab al-Tawasin*). Each of these short texts contained in its title the two Arabic letters *TA* and *SIN*, corresponding to *T* and *S*. This alphabet symbolism derives from the mysterious letters that are found at the beginning of certain books of the Qur'an (e.g., *TH* in book 20, or *YS* in book 36). The first of these texts, *The* TS *of the Lamp*, uses the metaphor of the lamp to symbolize the cosmic function of the Prophet Muhammad; his light (like a moon or star) is the first thing God created, and the entire universe exists through him. But it is through his historical mission in Arabia, recalled to Muslims by place names like Tahama and Yamama, and verified by followers such as Abu Bakr, that humanity receives the benefit of his spiritual authority. The Arabic style of Hallaj uses rhyming prose and wordplay to powerful effect, in a way that cannot be duplicated in English. Still, this piece is a good example of the way in which Sufis regarded the Prophet Muhammad as the central human figure in the drama of creation.

The *TS* of the Lamp
AL-HUSAYN IBN MANSUR AL-HALLAJ

A lamp appeared from the light of the hidden realm; it returned, and surpassed the other lamps, and prevailed. A moon manifested itself among the other moons. A star appeared, with a sign in the Heaven of secrets. God called Muhammad "illiterate" (Q 7:157) for his concentrated inspiration (which did not come from books), "man of the sanctuary" for the greatness of his fortune, and "Meccan" for his stability in nearness to God.

God opened his breast, raised his rank, enforced his command, and revealed his full moon. His full moon arose from the cloud of Yamama, and his sun dawned in the environs of Tahama, and his lamp radiated a mine of generosity.

He taught only from his own insight, and he commanded his example only by the beauty of his life. He was present before God and made God present, he saw and informed, he cautioned and warned.

No one has seen him in reality except his companion Abu Bakr the Confirmer. For he was in agreement with him, and then he was his companion, so that no division would occur between them.

No one really knew him, for all were ignorant of his true description. "Those to whom We gave the Book know Muhammad as they know their own sons, but there is a division among them, who conceal the truth although they know it" (Q 2:146).

The lights of prophecy emerged from his light, and his lights appeared from God's light. None of their lights is brighter, more splendid, or takes greater precedence in eternity, than the light of the Master of the Sanctuary.

His ambition preceded all other ambitions, his existence preceded nothingness, and his name preceded the Pen, because he existed before all nations and customs. There is not in the horizons, beyond the horizons, or below the horizons, anyone more elegant, more noble, more knowing, more just, more fearsome, or more compassionate, than the subject of this tale. He is the leader of created beings. His name is "glorious (Ahmad)," his nature is unique, his command is most certain, his essence is most excellent, his attribute is most illustrious, and his ambition is most distinctive.

How wonderful! How splendid, clear and pure, how magnificent and famous, how illuminated, capable, and patient he is! His fame was unceasing, before all created beings existed, and his renown was unceasing before there was any "before" and after any "after," when no substance or colors existed. His substance is pure, his word is prophetic, his knowledge is lofty, his expression is Arabic, his direction of prayer is "neither of the East nor the West" (Q 24:35), his descent is paternal, his peer Gabriel is lordly, and his companion Abu Bakr is maternally related.

Eyes have insight by his guidance, and inner minds and hearts attain their knowledge through him. God made him speak, God was the proof that confirmed him, and God dispatched him. He is the guide and he is the guided. He is the one who polished the rust from the mirror of the suffering breast. He is the one who brought an eternal Word, not temporal, not spoken, and not made, which is united with God without separation, and which passes beyond the understanding. He is the one who told of the end, and the ends, and the end of the end.

He lifted the clouds and pointed to the Sacred House. He is the perfect one, he is the magnanimous one, he is the one who ordered the idols to be smashed, he is the one who tore away the clouds, he is the one sent to all humanity, he is the one who distinguishes between honor and holiness.

Above him, a cloud flashed lightning, and beneath him, lightning flashed and sparkled. It rained and brought forth fruit. All sciences are but a drop from his ocean, all wisdom but a spoonful from his sea, all times are but an hour from his duration.

Truth exists through him, and through him reality exists; sincerity exists through him, and companionship exists through him. Chaos exists through him, and order exists through him (cf. Qur'an 21:30). He is "the first" in attaining union and "the last" in prophecy, "the outward" in knowledge "and the inward" in reality (Q 57:3).

No learned man has attained to his knowledge, and no sage is aware of his understanding.

God did not give him up to his creation, for he was He, as I am He, and He is He.

Never has anyone departed from the M of Muhammad, and no one has entered the H. His name contains an H and a second M, the D and the M at the beginning. The D is his remedy (*dawa'*), the M is his rank (*mahall*), the H is his spiritual state (*hal*), and the second M is his speech (*maqal*).

He revealed his proclamation, he displayed his proof, he caused the Criterion (the Qur'an) to descend, he made his tongue speak, he illuminated his paradises, he reduced his opponents to impotence, he established his edifice, he raised his dignity.

If you fled from his fields, then where would be the path, without any guide, you weak one? For the wisdom of the sages, next to his wisdom, is shifting sand.

* * *

The Prophet Muhammad as Moral Exemplar

IN CONTRAST to the poetic description of Hallaj, the section on the Prophet Muhammad in *The Book of Flashes* by Sarraj exhibits the same reliance on descriptive argument, with numerous quotations of scriptural passages, that he showed in his treatment of the Qur'an (see chapter 1, "Mystical Understanding of the Qur'an"). Here he naturally also recites numerous reports (*hadith*) of the sayings and deeds of the Prophet Muhammad, as related by oral transmission over the generations. Sarraj stresses how the Prophet Muhammad is recognized in the Qur'an for his moral and spiritual authority, but he also lays emphasis on the unpretentious and simple lifestyle that was characteristic of the Prophet. Many examples are given of the outstanding personal qualities of Muhammad, and devotion to the Prophet is signaled as one the key characteristics of the great Sufi masters. Sayings of famous Sufis about Muhammad are related by oral transmission ("I heard from so-and-so, who heard from so-and-so"), just as in the *hadith* reports of the Prophet. The frequent formulas of blessing that appear whenever the Prophet's name is mentioned are just one more example of the way in which reverence for Muhammad forms a basic part of Sufi practice.

The Book of the Example and Imitation of the Messenger of God

ABU NASR AL-SARRAJ

On the Character of the People of Purity, Understanding, Agreement, and on Following the Prophet (may God bless him and grant him peace)

The divine mission of Muhammad. God Most High said to the Prophet (may God bless him and grant him peace), "Say, 'People! I am the Messenger of God to all of you'" (Q 7:158). By that he taught us that he was sent to all humanity. Then He said, "You are guiding them by a straight path, the path of God; whatever is in the Heavens and on earth belongs to Him" (Q 42:52–53). Thus God Most High has borne witness to the Prophet, that he guides by a straight path. Then God requires us to reject the association of Muhammad's words with desire, because of the saying of God (He is great and powerful) "Muhammad does not speak from desire" (Q 53:3). God Most High then described him, saying, "He is the one who sent to the nations a messenger from among them, to recite to them His signs, to purify them, and to teach them the Book and wisdom" (Q 62:2). And God taught us that Muhammad recites to us God's signs and teaches us the Book, which is the Qur'an, and wisdom, that which is right. And the right is the Prophet's example, his manners, his morals, his deeds, his states, and his realities.

The authority of revelation and obedience to the Prophet. Then the Messenger of God (may God bless him and grant him peace) expressed what had been revealed to him by his Lord, which he was commanded to express, because of God's saying (He is great and powerful) "Messenger! Express what was revealed to you by your Lord" (Q 5:67). Then God (He is great and powerful) commanded all of humanity to obey the Messenger of God (may God bless him and grant him peace), as He commanded them to obey Himself, by God's saying (He is great and powerful) "Obey God, and obey the Messenger" (Q 24:54), and by God's saying (He is great and powerful) "Whoever obeys the Messenger has obeyed God" (Q 4:80). And God commanded them to accept Muhammad by God's saying (He is great and powerful) "Receive what the Messenger has brought you" (Q 59:7), and He commanded them to abstain from what the Prophet forbade by God's saying (He is great and powerful) "Abstain from what he forbids" (Q 59:7). He led them to guidance through following him, by God's saying (He is great and powerful) "Follow him, and perhaps you will be guided" (Q 7:158), and He promised them direction through obedience to him, by God's saying (He is great and powerful), "If you obey, you will receive direction" (Q 24:54). He warned them of disaster and severe punishment if they flouted his command, saying, "Let them beware, those who flout the Messenger's command, lest disaster or a severe punishment befall them" (Q 24:63). Then God Most High made us aware that the love of God for the believers, and the love of the believers for God, lies in obedience to His Messenger, by God's saying "Muhammad! Say, 'If you love God, obey me, and God will love you'" (Q 3:31). Then God assigned to the believers the beautiful example of His Messenger (may God bless him and grant him peace), saying, "There is a beautiful example for you in the Messenger of God" (Q 33:21).

The Prophetic tradition as model for behavior. Then reports were narrated from the Messenger of God (may God bless him and grant him peace), and each report descended from the Messenger (may God bless him and grant him peace), by transmission from one trustworthy person to another, until it reached us. Holding onto this is necessary for all of those who submit to God, by God's saying (He is great and powerful) "Offer prayer, give alms, and obey the Messenger" (Q 24:56), and God's saying (He is great and powerful), "Truly, Muhammad, you are on a straight path" (Q 43:43). Taking him as the example, following him, and obeying his command are necessary for all of His people, whether they bear witness or hide, until the Day of Resurrection. The only exception is for the three groups from whom the pen of destiny is lifted (sleepers, children, and the insane, none of whom are responsible for their actions).

Those who agree with the Qur'an, but do not follow the customs of the Messenger of God (may God bless him and grant him peace), actually contradict the Qur'an by not following him.

Following the Prophet in all things. Following and imitating means taking the "beautiful example" of the Messenger of God (may God bless him and grant him peace), in all that is correct in his morals, his deeds, his states, his commands, his prohibitions, his authorization, his encouragement, and his deterrence. The only exception is where there is direct evidence to the contrary, as in God's saying (He is great and powerful), "Exclusively for you, Muhammad, not for others who submit to God" (Q 33:50). Or as in the saying of the Messenger (may God bless him and grant him peace), "I am not like one of you," and his order to sacrifice, given to his uncle Abu Burda Niyar, "Sacrifice, and that will not be permitted to anyone after you," and similar direct evidence from text of scripture or tradition.

The Prophet as source of religious law. Now, what was narrated from the Messenger of God (may God bless him and grant him peace) regarding ordinances, injunctions, obligatory devotions, customs, commandments, prohibitions, recommendations, dispensations, and latitude, all concern the essentials of religion. It is recorded by the scholars and jurists and is applied by them in the course of their affairs. It is well known among them, because they are the leaders who preserve God's ordinances, who adhere to the customs of the Messenger of God (may God bless him and grant him peace). They are the supporters of God's religion (He is great and mighty), preserving people in their religion and explaining to them the difference between lawful and forbidden, true and false. They are the proofs of God Most High to His people, those who invite humanity on His behalf to His religion. They themselves are the elite among the masses.

Devotion to the example of the Prophet. And when the elite among those elite ones establish principles, preserve ordinances, and adhere to these customs, and nothing else remains to them that they should fulfill, then they investigate the reports of the Messenger of God (may God bless him and grant him peace), which have been transmitted regarding various acts of obedience, manners, devotions, noble characteristics, and pleasing conditions. They demand of themselves that they follow the Messenger of God (may God bless him and grant him peace) and take him as an example. They follow in his footsteps to the extent of their understanding of his manners, morals, deeds, and states, considering great what he considered great, and considering small what he considered small. They do seldom what he did seldom, and they do often what he did often. They hate what he hated, and they choose what he chose. They abandon what he abandoned, they endure what he endured, and they make a habit of what he made a habit. They adopt those whom he adopted, and they honor those whom he honored. They prefer what he preferred, and they are concerned about what concerned him. For when 'A'isha (may God be pleased with her) was asked about the character of the Messenger of God, she said, "His character was the Qur'an," meaning accordance with the Qur'an. It is also related that the Prophet (may God bless him and grant him peace) said, "I was sent with noble characteristics."

On Transmissions Concerning the Characteristics, Deeds, and States of the Prophet, Which God Chose for Him

Knowledge and humility. It was told of the Prophet (may God bless him and grant him peace) that he said, "God Most High instructed me in conduct, and He made my conduct beautiful." It was also told of him (may God bless him and grant him peace) that he said, "I know more of God than you, and I am in greater awe of God than you." It is correctly reported of the Messenger of God that he said, "I had to choose between being a prophet-king and a prophet-slave. Gabriel (peace be upon him) indicated to me that I should be humble, so I said, 'Yes, I shall be a prophet-slave, eating my fill one day and going hungry the next.' "

Poverty. It is told of him (may God bless him and grant him peace) that he said, "The world was offered to me but I refused it." He said (may God bless him and grant him peace), "If Mount Uhud were gold, I would spend it for the sake of God, except for a little I would set aside for debt." It is told of him (may God bless him and grant him peace) that he did not store anything for tomorrow, only once saving for a period of one year for his family, and for hosting anyone coming to him in a delegation.

It is told of him (may God bless him and grant him peace) that he did not own two shirts, and no bread was prepared for him. He departed from the world, never having had his fill of wheat bread—by choice, not by force. If he had asked God (who is great and mighty) to make him a mountain of gold without demanding an account, He would have done it. Similar things are told of him in reports and traditions.

Generosity. It is told of him (may God bless him and grant him peace) that he said to Bilal (may God be pleased with him), "Spend, Bilal, and do not fear any loss from God who is on the throne." Barira, a woman attached to Muhammad's wife 'A'isha, once placed before him food to eat. She brought him the same thing again the next night, and he said to her, "Did you not fear that there would be Hell-smoke in its place on the day of resurrection? Store nothing for tomorrow, for God Most High will bring sustenance every morning." Or he said, "For every day."

Unpretentiousness. It is told of him (may God bless him and grant him peace) that he never found fault with his food; if he wanted it, he ate, and if he didn't want it, he left it. Whenever he had to choose between two matters, he chose the easier. The Messenger of God (may God bless him and grant him peace) was not a farmer, a merchant, or a plowman. In his humility he dressed in wool, wore mended shoes, rode a donkey, milked the sheep, mended his own sandals, and patched his clothes. He did not disdain to ride a donkey, and he sat others behind him. It is told in tradition that he did not like wealth, he did not fear poverty, and he and his wives went for one or two months at a time without having kindled a fire in his house for bread. Their food was only "the two black things," dates and water.

His family. It is told of him that his women were given a

choice, and they chose God and his Messenger. It was in reference to them that the verses were revealed, "Prophet! Say to your wives, 'If you desire the life of this world and its adornment, come, I will compensate you and give you a fair alimony. But if you desire God, his Messenger, and the realm of the next world, God has prepared for the beneficent women among you a great reward' " (Q 33:28–29). One of his prayers (peace be upon him) was "God! Give me life as a beggar, let me die a beggar, and raise me up in the ranks of the beggars." Another of his prayers (may God bless him and grant him peace) was "God! Sustain the family of Muhammad with food from day to day."

Habits and character. Abu Sa'id al-Hudhri (may God be pleased with him) described the Messenger of God (may God bless him and grant him peace) in a tradition: The Messenger of God (may God bless him and grant him peace) used to hobble camels, fed the water-bearing camel, swept the house, mended sandals, patched clothes, milked sheep, ate with the servant, and ground flour with her when she lacked the strength. Modesty did not prevent him from bringing goods from the market for his family. He shook hands with rich and poor, and he was the first to give greeting. He did not reject anyone who asked him for something, and he did not belittle any request, even for the poorest dates. He had a gentle character, a noble nature, a cheerful face, and was wonderful company. He smiled without laughing, was sad without frowning, humble without abasement, and generous without waste. He had a gentle heart, kept his head bowed, and was compassionate to all who submitted to God. He never belched from fullness, and never stretched forth his hand in greed.

Generosity. 'A'isha (may God be pleased with her) said, "The Messenger of God (may God bless him and grant him peace) was more generous than the flowing wind." The Messenger of God gave all livestock found between two mountains to a single man. That man returned to his tribe, saying, "Muhammad (may God bless him and grant him peace) gives the gift of one who does not fear poverty." The Messenger of God was not noisy, shameless, or one who encouraged shamelessness. The Messenger of God ate on the earth, sat on the earth, dressed in a woolen cloak, joined the assembly of the poor, walked in the markets, laid his head on his hand, and exacted penalties on himself. He never laughed uncontrollably, never ate alone, and never struck a slave. He never hit anyone with his hand, except in war for God (who is great and mighty). He did not sit with crossed legs or eat reclining. He said, "I eat like a slave and sit like a slave." It is told of him that he tied a stone to his belly from hunger; this was at a time when, if he had asked his Lord to make Abu Qubays into gold for him, God would have done so. The Messenger of God took his companions to the house of Abu al-Haytham ibn Tayyahan without invitation, and in his house he ate his food and drank his drink. Muhammad said, "This is one of the bounties about which you will be able to report when you are questioned about your deeds on the Day of Resurrection." Another man invited him to his house, with five of his companions, and a sixth would not enter along with him without his permission.

Simplicity. It is related in tradition that the Messenger of God (may God bless him and grant him peace) once wore a shawl with designs on it during prayer. He threw it away, saying, "Its designs nearly distracted me." Then he said, "Bring me even the garment of my enemy Abu Jahm instead!" He was asked whether one can perform ritual prayer while wearing a single garment, and he said, "What? Have all of you managed to find two garments?" He said to a nervous questioner, "I am not a king; I am the son of a woman who used to eat dried camel meat." He said, "Do not consider me to be better than the prophet Jonah (peace be upon him), and do not give precedence to any of the prophets." Once he said, "I am the master of the sons of Adam, and that is no boast."

Concern for the poor. He said (may God bless him and grant him peace), "I give to some people, and others I deny, but those to whom I give are not dearer to me than those whom I deny." He said, "The first to enter Paradise will be the poor with unkempt heads and filthy clothes, who have not married women of luxury, for whom the barriers remain closed."

Suffering. He said, "What have I to do with the things of this world?" He said, "Let the sufficiency of any one of you rest on no more than the supplies of a rider." He said, "The poor of my community will enter Paradise a half day earlier than the rich, and that means five hundred years." He said, "We, the fellow prophets, suffer the most of all humanity; then come the most similar to us, and the next most similar. A man will suffer in proportion to his serving God. When his service is firm, the suffering is greatest."

Poverty. A man said to the Prophet, "I love you." He said,

"Prepare to wear suffering like a garment." It is related of the Prophet that he said, "Only three things from your world were made lovely for me." He also said, "You know your world better," connecting the world to them while he himself was departing from it. The Messenger of God (God bless him and grant him peace) never placed one brick on another up to the time he departed this world. When he left this world (peace be upon him), his armor was pawned to a Jew for a measure of barley, he left not a single coin, nor any inheritance to divide, and no furniture was found in his house. He said, "We fellow prophets do not bequeath anything; what we have left behind is our alms." He accepted gifts, favors, and presents, but he did not consume alms or accept them from others.

More on his poverty. It is told of him that he said (God bless him and grant him peace), "God did not inspire me to collect wealth and become a merchant, but He inspired me by saying, 'Recite the praise of your Lord, be one of those who bow in prostration, and worship your Lord until certainty comes to you' (Q 15:98–99)." It is transmitted from 'A'isha (peace be upon her) that she said, "We sacrificed a sheep, and we gave it away in alms until nothing remained but the shoulder blade. I said, 'Messenger of God! It's all gone but the shoulder blade.' The Prophet said, 'All of it remains except the shoulder blade!' " God (who is great and mighty) said, "N! By the pen, and what they write! You are not possessed, by the grace of God. There is a reward for you free of obligation, and you are a person of great character" (Q 68:1–4). And the Prophet (God bless him and grant him peace) said, "I was sent in order to perfect noble character."

His characteristics. Among his characteristics (God bless him and grant him peace) were modesty, liberality, trust in God, satisfaction, recollection, gratitude, gentleness, patience, forgiveness, pardoning, kindness, mercy, graciousness, counsel, peace, dignity, humility, indigence, generosity, munificence, submission, power, courage, friendship, sincerity, truthfulness, abstemiousness, contentment, complaisance, dread, respect, awe, prayer, weeping, fear, hope, protection, refuge, wakefulness, devotion, struggle, and striving.

Humility and steadfastness. And it is told of him (God bless him and grant him peace) that he was continually sad and always pensive, and in his breast there was a humming sound like a seething cauldron. He prayed until his feet swelled. He was asked, "Messenger of God! Have you not been forgiven 'your past and future sins' (Q 48:2)?" He said, "Am I not 'a grateful slave' (Q 17:3)?" He gave to those who refused him, and he joined with those who cut him off. He forgave those who wronged him, and he never took vengeance or got angry for his own sake, except that when the sacred ordinances of God were violated, that was something for which he grew angry. To widows he was like a sympathetic husband, and to orphans he was like a compassionate father.

Concern for others. He said (God bless him and grant him peace), "When goods are bequeathed they go to the heirs, but when neglected relatives are left they go to me." He said, "God! I am a man who gets angry like other men. If I have insulted or cursed any man, make that be his redemption," or however it was said. Anas ibn Malik said, "I served the Messenger of God for ten years, and he did not strike me or oppress me. He never said, when I did something, 'Why did you do it?' or when I didn't do something, 'Why didn't you do it?' "

Forbearance. If there had been no other example of his generosity, forgiveness, and forbearance except what he did on the day of the conquest of Mecca, that still would have been the height of perfection. That is because he entered in peace, though they had killed his uncles and his friends, after they had enclosed him in the ravines, punished his companions in various ways, expelled him, bloodied him, thrown dung on him, injured him and his companions, called him a fool, and gathered to deceive him. When he entered with no praise from them, and he overcame them in their worthlessness, he stood like a preacher and gave praise and adoration to God. He said, "I say what my brother Joseph (peace be upon him) said: 'There is no blame on you today, for God will forgive' (Q 12:92)." And he said, "Whoever enters the house of 'Abd Allah ibn Khafif Sufyan is safe." Similar things reported from authentic traditions on these topics are more numerous than one can repeat, and we have only mentioned a part as an indication of what we have not mentioned. And God knows best what is right.

On What Has Been Transmitted from the Messenger of God (God bless him and grant him peace) Regarding Dispensations and Exemptions That God Most High Permitted the Community, and Their Impact on the Imitation of the Messenger of God (God bless him and grant him peace) by the Elite and the Common

Prophetic dispensations for enjoying worldly goods. It is told of the Messenger of God (God bless him and grant him peace) regarding the goods that God collected for him from the defeated tribes of the Banu Qurayda, Nazir, Fadak, Khaybar, and the like—clothing given to him, the trunk, the sword in a silver scabbard, the curtains from the house, the flag that was his, the bow, the mule, the camel, the donkey, the cloak, the turban, the slippers given to him by the Ethiopian king, and other things too numerous to mention—that he used to love cold sherbet and ate date pudding. He said to his companions, "Eat your fill!" and similar things that have been reported in traditions about him. All of that concerns dispensation and exemption for the community, and permission for it, since he is the spiritual leader of the community until the Day of Judgment. He said (God bless him and grant him peace), "I was sent with the liberal religion of the one God." He also said, "I am only made to forget the standard of perfection so that I may be a practical model of behavior."

Worldly activities as concessions to human nature. Humanity would have perished if God Most High had not granted them dispensations and the appropriation of things that God permitted to them, in terms of desire, gathering, ownership, and acquisition, qualified by knowledge of religious law. This is because God Most High did not call them to gather goods, artifacts, and merchandise; rather, He permitted them that, for the sake of knowing Him, on account of their weakness. God Most High called them to obey Him and worship Him, and He assigned all the faithful to remember Him, thank Him, trust Him, and concentrate on Him. This is according to the saying of the Most High "You who believe! Remember God frequently" (Q 33:41), and the saying of the Most High "So trust in God, if you are faithful" (Q 5:23). The Transcendent One said, "I am your Lord, so worship Me" (Q 21:92), "be in awe of Me" (Q 2:40), "fear Me" (Q 2:41), and the like.

How prophets differ from ordinary people. The condition of the people in these permissions and dispensations is not like the condition of the prophets (peace be upon them), because the connection of most people to permissions and dispensations is from their weakness of faith, their selfish inclination toward pleasures, and their inability to bear the bitter weight of patience and contentment with what cannot be avoided. Often that leads them to follow desires and perform evil, if they fall short of their obligations and fail to stand by the demands of religious knowledge in their consumption. But the prophets (peace be upon them) have been corrected by the aid of prophecy, the power of being a messenger, and the illumination of revelation; things do not control them, since their engagement with things is for the sake of others, and their engagement with them is from their obligations, not from their desires. Have you not considered the saying of the Most High? "That which God bestows on His Messenger as tribute from the townsfolk is for God, for the Messenger, for relatives, orphans, beggars, and travelers" (Q 59:7). He thus indicates that what God bestows on the Messenger of God is for God and for the Prophet, for relatives and widows. It is said that "for the Messenger" means for the Messenger, so that he can put it in its proper place. And if anyone mentions "the one-fifth portion" of booty designated for the Prophet, that also he put where he wished.

Levels of spiritual status. People may be divided into three categories in terms of acceptance of the Book of God and following the Messenger of God (God bless him and grant him peace). There are those who are connected to dispensations, permissions, interpretation, and latitude. There are those who are connected to the knowledge of religious duties, exemplary practices, prohibitions, and commandments. And there are those who order those things, who know those portions of the commandments of religion for which ignorance provides no latitude. They are then connected to exemplary spiritual states, actions satisfying to God, noble character, lofty matters, the inner realities of obligations, realization, and sincerity, as transmitted in a report that the Prophet said to Harith: "Every truth has an inner reality. What is the reality of your faith?" He replied, "My soul has turned away from this world. I spend the night wakeful and the day thirsting. I seem to see my Lord manifest on the throne, and the people of Paradise visiting one another, and the people of Hell fighting each other." The Prophet said (God bless him and grant him peace), "You know indeed, so hold fast to your faith."

The Prophetic essence of Sufism. It is said that the essence of what is spoken of as esoteric knowledge is contained in four reports from the Prophet:

- the report of Gabriel (peace be upon him), when he asked the Messenger of God (God bless him and grant him peace) about submission to God (*islam*), faith, and virtue—"that you worship God as though you see Him";

- the report of 'Abd Allah ibn 'Abbas (may God be pleased with him), who said, "The Messenger of God (God bless him and grant him peace) took me by the hand and said, 'Remember God, and He will remember you' ";
- the report of Wabisa, "Sin is what injures your heart, and devotion is what gives peace to your soul";
- the report of Nu'man ibn Bashir from the Prophet (God bless him and grant him peace), "The lawful is clear, and the forbidden is clear," and the saying of the Prophet (God bless him and grant him peace), "There is no harming, nor retribution for harming, in Islam."

Tales of the Sufi Masters Who Are Distinguished for Following the Messenger of God (*God bless him and grant him peace*)

The Prophet's example as guide. I heard Abu 'Amr 'Abd al-Wahid ibn 'Alwan (may God have mercy on him) say, "I heard Junayd (may God have mercy on him) say, 'This knowledge of ours is woven of the reports of the Messenger of God (God bless him and grant him peace).' " I heard Abu 'Amr Isma'il ibn Nujayd say, "I heard 'Uthman Sa'id ibn 'Uthman al-Hiri say, 'One who commands himself to follow the exemplary behavior of the Prophet in word and deed speaks with wisdom, but one who commands himself to follow his own desire in word and deed speaks with heresy.' " God Most High said, "If you obey, you will receive direction" (Q 24:54).

Al-Bistami's reverence for the Prophet. I heard Tayfur al-

Bistami say, "I heard Musa ibn 'Isa (known as 'Umayya) say, 'I heard my father say, "I heard Abu Yazid al-Bistami (may God have mercy on him) say, 'Come with us, so we may see this man who has proclaimed his own sainthood.' In his neighborhood, the man was sought out and famous for his asceticism and devotion. Tayfur told us his name, but I forgot it. We went there, and when he came out of his house and entered the mosque, he spat in the direction of Mecca. Abu Yazid said, 'Come with us, let us leave.' He left without greeting the man, saying, 'This man is not trustworthy regarding the practice of the Messenger of God (God bless him and grant him peace), so how could he be trustworthy regarding the spiritual stations of the saints and sincere ones that he claims?' " I heard Tayfur say, "I heard Musa ibn 'Isa say, 'I heard my father say, "I heard Abu Yazid say (may God have mercy on him), 'I planned to ask God Most High for a sufficient supply of food and women, but then I thought, "How can it be permissible for me to ask God Most High for this, when the Messenger of God (God bless him and grant him peace) did not?" So I did not ask for it, and God gave me a sufficient supply of women, so that I no longer care whether it is a woman or a wall that is in front of me,' " or however he said it.

Deathbed reverence. I heard Abu al-Tayyib Ahmad ibn Muqatil al-'Akki al-Baghdadi say, "I was with Ja'far al-Khuldi (may God have mercy on him) the day that al-Shibli died. Bakran al-Dinawari came, who was the servant of al-Shibli (may God have mercy on him) and had been present at his death. Ja'far asked him, 'What did you see from him at the time of his death?' He said, 'When his tongue was stilled, and his brow sweated, he gestured to me to perform his ablutions for ritual prayer. But I forgot to comb his beard according to the Prophet's custom, and he seized my hand and ran my fingers through his beard to comb it.' Ja'far cried, and said, 'What can one say about a man who does not forget about combing his beard, in the death agony of his spirit, when his tongue is stilled and his brow sweating?' " or however it was said.

Sufi devotion to the Prophet. I heard Ahmad ibn 'Ali al-Wajihi say, "I heard Abu 'Ali al-Rudhbari say, 'My master in the science of Sufism was Junayd, my master in Islamic law was Abu al-'Abbas ibn Surayj, my master in grammar and lexicography was Tha'lab, and my master in the reports of the Messenger of God (God bless him and grant him peace) was Ibrahim al-Harbi." Dhu al-Nun (may God have mercy on him) was asked, "How did you come to know God Most High?" He said, "I knew God by God, and everything else I knew by the Messenger of God (God bless him and grant him peace)." Sahl ibn 'Abd Allah (may God have mercy on him) said, "Every ecstasy to which the Holy Book and the Prophetic example does not bear witness is worthless." Abu Sulayman al-Darani (may God have mercy on him) said, "Sometimes my heart knocks on the door of reality for forty days, but I only permit my heart to enter it with two witnesses, one from the Holy Book and one from the Prophetic example."

Conclusion. This is what comes to me at the moment about the attitude of the Sufis toward following the Messenger of God (God bless him and grant him peace). I hate to be overly long, so for convenience I shortened what I recalled. And success is from God.

3

SPIRITUAL PRACTICE

I T MIGHT BE SAID that spiritual practice is the core of
Sufism. Theories and metaphysical points of view have
certainly been elaborated by Sufi writers, but it is in meditation, prayer, fasting, and other day-to-day practices that
we find the life of this mystical path. A great many Sufi
writings, in fact, treat these kinds of practices in detail.
This is particularly true of the meditative practices associated with the "recollection" (*dhikr*) of the names of God.
Literature on mystical practice increasingly became available in Persian as well as Arabic during the eleventh and
twelfth centuries. The selections that follow cover a range
of practices, and they illustrate how specialization tended
to become noticeable over the centuries, as particular Sufi
orders developed distinctive techniques.

CONDITIONS OF THE SPIRITUAL PATH

ONE OF THE MOST influential figures in the development
of Sufism was Najm al-Din Kubra (d. 1220), after whom the
Kubrawi Sufi order takes its name. Like his successor 'Ala'
al-Dawla Simnani (see chapter 7), Kubra was greatly con-

cerned with training disciples, and he left a number of treatises designed for practical spiritual instruction. *The
Bewildered Traveler* is a short Persian text that Kubra wrote
at the request of some disciples who found his Arabic writings difficult. The sections translated below cover the topics of silence, fasting, seclusion, recitation of the first half
of the Muslim profession of faith ("There is no god but
God"), and control of thoughts. Other topics discussed in
this text include purity, keeping good company, avoiding
sleep, and control of eating and drinking. The format consists of brief numbered observations on the benefits of each
practice, with frequent references to the Qur'an and the
life of the Prophet Muhammad. This is a good example of a
basic Sufi text on spiritual practice, intended for beginners.

from *The Bewildered Traveler*
Najm al-Din Kubra

*Silence of the External Tongue, Except for
Recollection of God Most High*

In silence of the external tongue, eleven benefits are evident:

1. Release from the reckoning on Resurrection Day.
2. When the external tongue is silent, the tongue of the
   heart begins to speak.
3. Salvation from Hell, for the Messenger (peace be upon
   him) said, "Will anything cast people into Hell, on their

faces or on their noses, except for the harvest of their tongues?"

4. Every day, the bodily limbs all demand of the tongue, "Be silent from excessive speech," for if it does not speak, it is healthy for their parts.

5. The carnal soul is disciplined by silence, for this carnal soul is an idle talker.

6. If one is silent, it may be that one hears the speech of angels, for as the Prophet said, "God speaks by the tongue of 'Umar and his heart."

7. Treasures of wisdom are opened for him, for the Messenger (peace be upon him) said, "When you see a man of long silence, sit with him, for he will teach you wisdom."

8. He says in a similitude, "If speech is silver, silence is gold."

9. In silence there is a resemblance to Zacharias (peace be upon him), for God Most High told him, "The sign for you shall be that you do not speak to the people for three days, except by ciphers" (Q 3:41). And when Zacharias did not speak for three days, God Most High made John the Baptist speak during the days of his infancy. It is no wonder if, when a man of the path is silent for a few days, the John of his heart will speak at the beginning of his path.

10. There is a resemblance to Mary (prayers and peace be upon her), the mother of Jesus (peace be upon him), for she said, "I dedicated my fasting to the Merciful One, and I will not speak to any person today" (Q 19:26). When she chose silence, God Most High

made Jesus speak as a baby, saying, "I am the servant of God, who brought me the Book" (Q 19:35). It is no wonder that, when the man of the path is silent from all spoken words, the Jesus of his heart begins to speak.

11. In silence, there is continuous recollection of God Most High by heart and tongue. In the Prophet's words, "For the people of Paradise there will be no greater sorrow in Paradise than that moment that befell them in the world when they did not recite the recollection of God Most High or the adoration of the Prophet."

Constant Seclusion and Isolation from the People

On this topic there are at least twelve additional benefits:

1. Protecting the sight from gazing with desire.
2. Protecting the foot from walking toward the forbidden.
3. Protecting the hand from taking and receiving the forbidden.
4. Protecting the ear from hearing the forbidden.
5. Binding and confining the carnal soul.
6. When the external senses are shut off, the internal senses, which are the doors of the hidden world, are opened.
7. Being far away from the annoyances of the people.
8. Choosing well-being, for it is said, "Well-being is in solitude."
9. Resembling spiritual beings, for the people do not see them.

10. Attaining concentration of the heart.

11. Gaining the level of the shadow of the throne of the Merciful One. As the Messenger said, "There are seven people whom God protects with His shadow on the day when there will be no shadow except the shadow of God's throne." One of them is "the man who remembers God while in seclusion, and tears fall from his eyes."

12. Banishing from the heart the images of the world and the practices, the giving, and the taking of worldly people. When the face of one's heart is purified of the images of the world, the images of the next world strike sparks in the heart. When it becomes purer, spiritual states and realities strike sparks in the heart, and when it becomes purer still, the attributes of God Most High strike sparks in it by way of reflection. When its purity becomes perfect, unity strikes sparks in it, so that it takes away soul, intellect, and consciousness. Then divine knowledge is attained, and one joins the people of manifestation.

Fasting

Fasting has twenty-two benefits:

1. Resemblance to spiritual beings, for they eat none of the things we eat.

2. Overpowering the carnal soul that commands evil, for it is the enemy of God Most High.

3. Attaining distinction; the Prophet reported that God said, "Fasting is Mine, and I provide the reward for it."

4. Getting an infinite reward, for "the patient obtain their recompense without reckoning" (Q 39:15).

5. Purifying the filthy carnal soul from sins.

6. Washing the psychic dirt from the seed of the pure soul so that the images of the knowledge of the divine presence become clear, for "one who purifies it succeeds, and one who adulterates it fails" (Q 91:9–10).

7. Banishing the cataracts that afflict the eye of the heart. When a man is hungry, the glaucoma in the eye of the heart goes away. The eye of the heart becomes clear, it looks on the hidden world, and it beholds the angelic realm.

8. Closing off the roads to Satan, which are the veins in the body, because Satan goes in the vein and skin.

9. Getting a shield against Satan and Hell, for "fasting is Paradise."

10. Fixing one's name in the roster of the sincere ones, because fasting is a devotion in which hypocrisy and showing off do not fit.

11. Understanding the suffering of the hungry, and forgiving them by way of compassion and mercy.

12–13. Attaining two kinds of happiness. One happiness is at the time of breaking a fast, not because one wishes to eat bread, but because for a single day one has kept the fast for the sake of satisfying God Most High; until Resurrection Day, this will be his achievement. The other happiness is to see God Most High on Resurrection Day.

14. Attaining bodily health.

15. Emptying the worst of containers, for "no full container is worse than the belly."

16. Deserving trust, for fasting is the trust of God Most High; no other person is aware of the faster except God.

17. Keeping the promise, for when the faster makes a vow, "I will fast," this is a promise that he has made to God Most High.

18. Being entrusted with a rank for oneself, for the Messenger said, "The faster is a volunteer for the commander of his soul"; that is, he is trusted.

19. Writing good in one's account. If one can complete the fast, one writes 100 percent good, and if it is not completed, still one writes 10 percent, from the promise of the Messenger (peace be upon him), "The intention of the believer is more serious than his action." If the action has such excellence that when one attains completion with sincerity, one writes 100 percent, nevertheless there is still the danger that when hypocrisy and showing off intrude, the fasting will just be a bluff. But with pure intention this is not the case, because intention is the action of the heart. Angels are not aware of it; it is restricted to humanity. Thus there is no room in it for hypocrisy and showing off.

20. Avoiding silly and foolish speech.

21. According to the promise of the Messenger (peace be upon him), "foolish talk is not counted against a faster after his next prayer."

22. The faster receives aid and help, for "they seek aid through fasting and prayer."

Constant Recollection of "There is no god but God"

If one also frequently says, "Muhammad is the Messenger of God," that is very good. The knowledge of the ancients and the moderns is contained in this phrase.

> When you remember God, you get Him.
> Otherwise, it's like trying to grab the wind.
> Those evils you've committed with heart and soul—
> Leave them alone; you've paid for them all.

Since I said that the knowledge of the ancients and the moderns is contained in this phrase, explaining its benefits would be superfluous.

> Putting a garment on the Ka'ba is vanity.
> The "My" of "My house" is all the beauty the Ka'ba needs.

After all this, some benefits will be mentioned.

1. The Messenger (peace be upon him) said, "I was commanded to fight the people until they said, 'There is no god but God, Muhammad is the Messenger of God.' And when they said that, their lives and property were safe from me, except by God's right. And their accounting is with God Most High."
2. It is the highest of the seventy-seven signs of faith, for the Prophet said that "the loftiest of them is the testimony that there is no god but God."
3. Whoever once honestly says, "There is no god but God," and then dies, will go to Heaven.

4. The Messenger (peace be upon him) said, "The key to Paradise is 'There is no god but God.'"

5. The Messenger (peace be upon him) said, "One who knows that there is no god but God will enter Paradise."

6. It is this saying that they lift up with their voices, for "good words ascend to Him, and He exalts the righteous deed" (Q 35:10).

7. The greatest name of God (Allah) is in this saying.

8. When the devotee says, "There is no god but God," the pillars quake on the throne of God Most High. God Most High says, "Throne, be still." And the throne says, "How can I be still, when you have not forgiven the one who has spoken?" And God Most High says, "Be still, for I have forgiven him."

9. This saying is the most excellent of recollections, for "the most excellent recollection is 'There is no god but God.'"

10. The most excellent saying that any of the messengers and prophets (peace be upon them) have ever said is this saying, "There is no god but God, He alone, He has no partner."

11. This saying is a recollection of God and an affirmation of God's unity, but not every recollection of God affirms His unity.

12. This saying is the negation and affirmation. It is the negation of false gods, and the affirmation of God Most High.

13. As long as infidels do not repeat this saying, they cannot become Muslims.

14. This is the saying of salvation, and if there were a saying that were better than this for salvation, the Messenger (peace be upon him) would have spoken it to his uncle Abu Talib.

15. The Messenger (peace be upon him) became angry with Usama, who was his client and friend, because an infidel in the midst of battle had said, "There is no god but God," and Usama had struck him. So Muhammad said, "Do you not give anyone credit for saying, 'There is no god but God'? Have you killed him after he said, 'There is no god but God'?"

16. One day the companions of the Messenger (peace be upon him) said, "So-and-so is a hypocrite." The Messenger (peace be upon him) said, "So you say, but in the end isn't he someone who has said, 'There is no god but God'?" They said, "Yes, Messenger of God." He said, "Every devotee who honestly says, 'There is no god but God,' will enter Paradise."

17. When the devotee recites, "There is no god but God," he fills Heaven and earth, that is, he fills the balance in the scales of judgment.

18. On Resurrection Day, they will bring the devotee to the plains of judgment, and they will weigh his good and evil. If his evil tips the scale, God Most High will say to him, "Don't you have any more good?" He will say, "Lord, I don't." And then he will lose hope. God Most High will say, "But you do have something beautiful relating to Me." If he had once said, "There is no god but God," they will bring it written on a piece of paper the size of a fingernail. This devotee will see that

the levels of his sins are many, and he will see the amount of one fingernail-sized piece of paper, and he will say, "Lord, what is the value of this fingernail in comparison with those records?" God Most High will say, "There is no injustice today." Then they will place the piece of paper the size of a fingernail in one pan of the balance and the records of evil in the other pan. When those records of evil fly up like the wind, and the other pan becomes heavy with the paper saying, "There is no god but God," they will take him to Paradise. The transmitter of this Prophetic saying says, "In that assembly where they recited this account, there was a poor man whom no one knew. When he heard this account, a cry came forth from him, and in the midst of that cry he gave up his soul. The scholars there prepared him for burial, and I was there and prayed for him."

If I had wished to, I would have mentioned a thousand excellences and benefits of this saying, but I thought it more appropriate to summarize to this extent.

The Denial of Thoughts

This is the most difficult condition for the wayfarers on the path to God Most High. The reality of the denial of thoughts is the reality of recollection, because thoughts are of five kinds:

The first is the thought that is from God, and the sign of that thought is that it enters the heart spontaneously, and one should not deny that thought. In reality, one cannot do so, but that is the practice of beginners, that they do deny it, because the beginner has not yet distinguished it from the thoughts that come from the master.

The second is the thought from the heart, and the third is the thought from the angel. These two are close to each other, yet between the thought from the heart and the thought from the angel there is a subtle difference. You will know this difference from the situation of the Messenger (peace be upon him). He was chivalrous, in the month of Ramadan he was more chivalrous, and when Gabriel (peace be upon him) was near, he was still more chivalrous. So you realize that, from the presence of the angel and his thoughts, chivalry is increased.[1]

Fourth is the thought from the carnal soul. Fifth is the thought from Satan. These two thoughts are close to one another, but between the two thoughts there is a difference. That is, when the carnal soul desires something and does not get it, it continues to desire it. In the desire for that thing, conflicts appear. But when Satan commands something that is a sin, if a man does not do it, Satan wants him to do something else, for his goal is to mislead. Another difference between the thought from the heart and the angel on the one hand, and the thought from the carnal soul and Satan on the other, is that the thoughts from the heart and the angel seek nearness to God Most High, and

---

[1] The author refers here to the Islamic ethical code of chivalry (Arabic *futuwwa*, Persian *javanmardi*), which was widely followed both in Sufi orders and in civic associations.

they incline toward the satisfaction of God Most High and the attainment of the reward of the next world. The carnal soul and Satan avoid nearness to God Most High, and they incline toward worldly vanities and passionate desires. Another difference is that the thoughts from the angel and the heart produce peace and quietude of the heart without internal objection. But in the thoughts of the carnal soul and Satan, an internal heaviness appears, and from every corner objections appear. Another difference is that the heart and the angel desire all that is praiseworthy in all circumstances, while the carnal soul and Satan desire all that is blameworthy in all circumstances. Another difference is that the thought of the heart and the angel are in agreement with the Book of God and the example of the Messenger (peace be upon him), while the thought of the carnal soul and Satan are in conflict with the Book of God, with the heart, with the angel, and with the example of the Messenger (peace be upon him). Another difference is that the thought of the angel and the heart increases certainty, but from the thought of the carnal soul and Satan, doubt and deception enter. Another difference is that the thought of the angel and the heart are of the type of thought that is near the moment of death, and the thought of the carnal soul and Satan is of the kind of thought that appears at the time of bodily health and happiness. Another difference is that at the time of the thought of the angel and the heart, witnessing becomes more pure and obscurity departs, while the thought of the carnal soul and Satan has no other character than obscurity and heaviness of heart.

* * *

MEDITATIONS OF THE
SHATTARI ORDER

THE GREAT SOCIAL extension of the Sufi orders began to take place around the twelfth century, and particular lineages took on the names of the major saints regarded as their founders. One of the orders that emerged somewhat later was the Shattari order, named after 'Abd Allah Shattari (d. 1428). From its origins in Central Asia and Iran, it flourished in India, where Shattari leaders were closely associated with the royal dynasty of the Mughals. Later on, the Shattari orders spread to Southeast Asia and the Arabian peninsula. This particular order was characterized by an intense interest in the formulas of meditation, which even included non-Arabic divine names from Persian and Hindi. The texts translated here are characteristic examples of Shattari practice, emphasizing the recitation of the divine names, the manifestation of divine qualities in the human form, and meditative techniques of breath control and visualization. The first two are short works bound together in a single volume, both written by Shah 'Isa Jund Allah (d. 1622), a Sufi master who lived in western India in Burhanpur. Although the copy used for translation was incomplete, lacking the opening page and one other passage of *The Treatise on Meditation*, these texts are of special interest because of the concentrated form of meditation technique employed and because of the unusual illustrations that accompany them (figures 1–12, pages 59–69). These illustrations consist of calligraphic representations of the human face and figure, composed of the Arabic letters that spell the names Muhammad (محمد), ʿAli (علي), and God (Allah, الله). These names are symmetrically arranged, both in their normal form and in a mirror image, around a vertical axis through the center of the face. Generally (figures 1–3, 6–8), the name of ʿAli (inverted) forms the eyes, nose, and ears, while the name of Muhammad is arranged to form the mouth and cheeks (and occasionally the body). The name Allah appears in two of these illustrations in the place of the heart. These figures belong to a familiar type of representation associated with the cabalistic Hurufi sect, which sought to understand the secret of the universe from the letters of the Arabic alphabet. Similar figures can be found particularly in the art of the Bektashi Sufis in Turkey and southeastern Europe.

The texts themselves are esoteric, and would require significant explanation from a qualified master to be fully comprehensible. They are expressed in terms of a complex cosmology and metaphysics based upon standard themes in Sufi thought, such as the three levels of truth (religious law, spiritual path, and reality), the three aspects of the human being (spirit, heart, and body), the names of God, and the doctrine that the human body is a microcosm or miniature equivalent of the entire universe. Other topics are more specialized, including a version of the doctrine of the emanation of the cosmos in the Five Presences, which derives from the school of Ibn ʿArabi. The first of these works, *The Treatise on Meditation*, focuses on the structure of the cosmos and its relation to the form of the human body, particularly the face. The second work, *The Treatise on the Intermediate State*, by its title refers to the Prophet

Muhammad as the intermediary or isthmus who connects the realms of the divine and the human. The bulk of it is occupied with the description of four meditative exercises in recollection (*dhikr*), the chanted recitation of the names of God, and breath control. These texts contain detailed instructions for visualization, with accounts of the presiding archangels and other associations (such as parts of the body or colors) for each recollection. Both of these writings are based on the concept of the Perfect Human (*al-insan al-kamil*) as the being who comprehensively unites all levels of existence.

The Treatise on Meditation
'ISA JUND ALLAH

The three levels of truth. . . . One encounters his own master, either in person or at a distance. When this becomes established in the heart, he then concentrates on having the same kind of encounter with the revered Prophet (may God bless him and grant him peace). When this too becomes natural, he attains "the encounter with his Lord, so let him act rightly" (Q 18:110). "Acting rightly" here means meditation, which is just like "presence" in the saying "There is no real ritual prayer without presence of the heart." This is on the first level, that of the religious law. In the religious law, only presence is established in the heart, and witnessing and quietude follow. When one attains witnessing, vision takes place; this is described by the saying, "The Prophet is totally absorbed in ritual prayer." This process takes place on all three levels: in the religious law (*shari'at*), on the spiritual path (*tariqat*), and in the spiritual reality (*haqiqat*).

Political and spiritual authority of the Prophet. On the topic of witnessing, the revered Prophet said, "One who has seen me has seen God." The explanation is as follows. In the Holy Scripture, it is said, "Obey God, obey the Messenger, and those who hold authority" (Q 4:59). In the religious law, "those who hold authority" means the ruler, who is called the interpreter of the religious law. On the spiritual path, he is called a master. It is a religious duty to carry out both these forms of authority. This authority is of two types, external and internal. External authority is the religious law, which everyone carries out. Internal authority is the spiritual path, which the masters enact, and this authority does not reach perfection except through meditation, which is being in the divine presence.

Spirit, heart, and body, and the three levels of truth. All the wayfarers and upholders of God's unity say that there are three meanings in the Qur'anic verse just quoted: (1) "Obey God" is the station of the spirit. (2) "Obey the Messenger" is the station of the heart. The bodily form of the divine essence is fixed in the heart, but it is veiled from the five senses. It sees without the eye, hears without the ear, and speaks without the tongue. The inner divine archetype is hidden from the outer senses. The heart is its roof material, comparable to a canopy over a throne, for "the heart of the believer is the canopy of God Most High." (3) "Those who hold authority" is the station of the body, and the body is the station of the religious law. The action of this station is performed with bodily limbs. But the station of the spiritual path is the heart, and the action of its station is performed by meditation. On the level of reality, all is spirit, and this is not even attained by annihilation in annihilation. Here, understanding is impotent and imagination fails. This station is not easily attained except through perfect love, for it is the station of the spirit. One obtains this authority by the vision of realities. Here there is universal understanding, so that one truly knows.

Divine attributes and the emanation of the human form. The spirit is in the form of the body. These are the three levels of the descent of the divine essence (spirit, heart, and body). (1) The spirit exists in the station and level of absolute singleness. (2) The heart is in the secret reality of unity and in the station of unity, but absolute singleness is higher than unity. (3) Part of the spark of the light of the divine essence, the seven chief names of God that they call the "seven mothers," manifested itself in the bodily form of Muhammad and Adam. The light of Muhammad simultaneously illuminated all things through these seven chief names of God: Knowing, Hearing, Seeing, Speaking, Willing, Living, and Powerful. It was to that bodily form that Muhammad alluded by saying, "I was a prophet when Adam was between water and clay." The "seven mothers" descended into existence through the Five Presences (i.e., God's essence, the spiritual world, the imaginal world, the bodily world, and the Perfect Human). Necessarily, when these descend from the divine presence, they are five. The descents of Muhammad, the Perfect Human, are in the hidden realm of the divine essence, but his appearance is by means of the spirit, the imaginal, and the bodily. As one master has said, "The fifth presence (i.e., the Perfect Human) comprehends these other presences." If one has this vision by lofty insight and manifestation, where can intellectual understanding fit, except in the perfect, comprehensive, and practicing knower of God? Sayyid Niʿmat Allah has said:

> Since I saw Your beauty in manifestation,
> I saw and witnessed the Beloved's face.
> Then I looked upon the seeing eye,
> And I saw a bodily form as essential meaning.

Visualizing the Perfect Human in the human face. One visualizes the intermediate state of Muhammad in three parts of one's face. One pictures the pupil of the right eye as the presence of divine singularity. One looks at the nose, which is the intermediate state, as the presence of the unity of Muhammad. One takes the pupil of the left eye as one's revered master. All three diagrams come together in this fashion [see figures 1 and 2].

The eye that sees the beauty of the Prophet sees the world of purity. You must know with certainty that wherever one gazes upon the beauty of the Prophet, one sees God. This is shown in the third diagram that is drawn here [see figure 3].

The lords of the spiritual path and the companions of reality call this picture "two bow's lengths" (Q 53:9, measuring the distance separating Muhammad from God at the height of Muhammad's ascension). They call this "two bow's lengths," because the spiritual path is in the form of

FIGURES 1 *and* 2. *Two depictions of the Perfect Human in the human face. Each is composed of the Arabic calligraphy for the names of Muhammad and 'Ali.*

FIGURE 3. *"Two bow's lengths"* *(Qur'an 53:9).*

two bows, the bow of God, whose existence is necessary, and the bow of creation, whose existence is merely possible. The two bows are the two eyes, together with the intermediate state of Muhammad, which is the nose, for the human face is not right without the nose. The levels of the two bows that appear in the human face have two "prayer niches" (*mihrab*s, i.e., the eyebrows) above them.

Divine structure of the face. It is also known that the form of the human face is like two compasses that make the circles of the eyes; one belongs to the divine essence, and the other to the divine attributes. Both compasses have closed their circles, the form of the face is structured in levels, and the two bows meet in one point. The right side belongs to the divine essence, and the left side to the divine attributes. If you imagine this, you will know the human face as the veil of Divinity [see figure 4]. "Humanity is my secret and my attribute." The essence has been discovered. God said, "We are closer to humanity than the jugular vein" (Q 50:16). The words of the Prophet are clear: "You will see your Lord on Resurrection Day as though you saw the full moon." Without recognition of the face, there is no divine knowledge. If someone's head is separated from his body, no one can recognize his body. When one sees the face, one recognizes the person, because the light of the divine essence manifests itself from the heart in the face, so that it is evident to the senses; vision, hearing, and speech are part of that. It is written in the Holy Scripture, "That day their faces will be shining, gazing at their Lord" (Q 75:22–23). The subtle divine body is visible, but it is not seen by the vision of mundane existence.

The human being as the microcosm. Thus the divine decree is interpreted in the human body through the four elements, by its own universal command. From the navel upward is the celestial station, and from the navel downward is the nether station; the entire form of the Heavens is in the human being. "Humanity is the construction of the Lord" is firmly established; God is the meaning. God said, "God is with you wherever you are" (Q 57:4). The divine essence is discovered.

> If you had no eye, still you would know
> That we have put a jewel before a blind man.
> When we sent Adam out of Paradise,
> We kept our beauty in the wilderness.

FIGURE 4. *The human face as the veil of Divinity.*

When the seeker persists and continues, both in scarcity and plenty, by day and night, he should remember, when he is settled in his heart and vision, that the outcome of "Perhaps you will see God visibly in this world" will appear. "Perhaps you will give thanks" (Q 2:52) will provide guidance. "God will provide assistance."

Seeker! In the practice of spiritual states, and the attainment of perfection, let me explain the form of the Heavens that is in humanity [see figure 5]. The circle of the head is like Heaven, and the two eyes are like the sun and moon. The zenith is like the teeth . . . [*gap in text*]

. . . sparkled in the heart, and in the brain the senses became illuminated from that. God Himself said, "The Merciful One is seated on the throne" (Q 20:5). The saying of God that Muhammad reported, "God created Adam in His own form" [see figure 6], is the secret of this meaning.

The spirit is from the sparkling lights of manifestation,

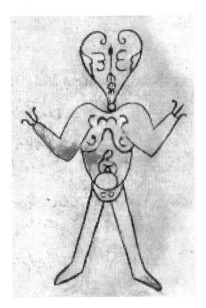

FIGURE 5. *"The form of the heavens that is in humanity."*

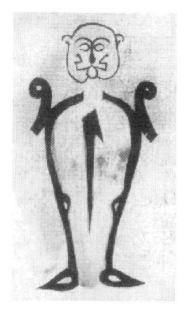

FIGURE 6. *"God created Adam in His own form." The limbs and body of the figure are formed by the name Muhammad, with the* Alif (A) *for* Allah *in the center.*

and the One itself comes from within quietude. As in the saying of God Most High, "God is the light of the Heavens and the earth" (Q 24:35). The meaning of "Heavens" is the spirit, and the meaning of "earth" is the body [see figure 7]. There are two gross and two subtle substances among the four elements, as Shaykh Farid al-Din 'Attar says (God have mercy on him):

FIGURE 7. *God is the light of the body.*

He created the body from earth and water,
He blew air and fire into the spirit.

By saying to Muhammad, "I fermented the clay of Adam for forty days with both My hands," God announced the sealing of this lesson, and "I blew My spirit into him" (Q 15:29) attained its goal. The angels prostrated themselves.

If a spark of God had not come into existence,
How would angels prostrate before flesh and blood?
That giver of wisdom whose essence is Adam—

All His wonders were known in scripture.
Everything hidden was revealed by Him—
It was this meaning that became the outward forms.
Gaze at the very forms of what you see.
Go beyond creatures, see the all as God.
When that One without quality gave peace to qualified
   existence,
Beneath its veil, he called it Joseph.
The sun has gone into the veil of humanity.
Understand this, though God knows best.

The Treatise on the Intermediate State
'Isa Jund Allah

Whoever grasps the meaning of this treatise does not retain any of the limitations of either the worshiper or the worshiped. If he prays in a mosque, if he prostrates himself before idols in a temple, it is the same relationship. As Shaykh Shabistari states in *The Rose Garden of Mystery*:

If the infidel were aware of infidelity,
How could he go astray in his religion?
If Muslims knew what the idol was,
They would know that true religion is in idolatry.

Visualizing the name of God in the heart. Know that the heart is the station of earthiness and also the stage of divinity; it is the level of reality, the station of the spirit, the station of love, the station of intellect, and the station of

FIGURE 8. *The names of 'Ali and Muhammad form the face; "Allah" is contained in the heart.*

the carnal soul. It is also called "the praiseworthy station" (Q 17:79); that is, the essence of God Most High manifests itself in it. The bodily form of the name of the divine essence is in the heart [see figure 8]. That is, one conceives the word *God* (*Allah*) with a white color, or a gold color, in the heart. In the world of witnessing, one beholds it through fancy and imagination on the page of the heart, and one sees with the eye of the spirit the form of the word *God*. With a hidden tongue, the heart begins recollecting, as they have stated. The intermediate state, the divine essence, the divine attributes, and the physical qualities of extension, intensification, above, and below appear. Seeker! For you, every soul has the experience of longing.

Four Practices of Recollection

1. The recollection of the seven mothers. The means to the divine essence is the word *God*, and the means to the divine attributes are the eight primary attributes: essence, life, knowledge, will, power, hearing, speech, and sight. These eight levels also have an external and an internal implication; you are all of these. The seven chief divine names—Hearing, Seeing, Willing, Speaking, Living, Powerful, and Knowing—all announce these attributes. In one breath one causes the word *Allah* to ascend and descend, with the inner gaze focused, extending the A of *Allah* at length, and pronouncing the L intensively, drawing the word upward and downward, from beneath the navel upward. This recollection is called "the recollection of the seven mothers." One performs this recollection with reflection; that is, one reflects on the shape of the word *God*. This station has a doorkeeper. When one has presented the password for this station, one sees that the overseer of this station is Gabriel (peace be upon him). It is white in color. Know that this is the station of water; it is the station of divine knowledge, the stage of power, and the source of the water of life. They lead within, ever within, to the top of the triple compass of the brain [figure 9]. In the middle of that triple compass of the brain, the source of the water of

life appears. It is the court of the spirit. One sees the form of the spirit reflected in that water, as one sees the moon in the water.

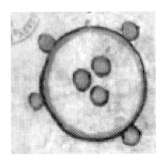

FIGURE 9. *The triple compass of the brain.*

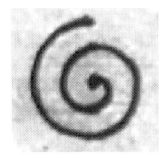

FIGURE 10. *The circle of the navel.*

2. The recollection of the secret and the existence of the Creator. They lead within. The cry "He, He" (*Hu, Hu*) is heard. They call this recollection "the secret and the existence of the creator." The doorway to the next station is the two eyes. Three of the eight primary divine attributes are in this station: Hearing, Seeing, and Knowing. The overseer of this station is Michael (peace be upon him), and this station is called "the defending emperor." The sign of this station is the liver. It has a green color. Know that the stomach is the station of memory. From the circle of the navel, the wind rises to the level of the spiritual path; it is at the station of the angelic realm. [See figure 10.]

3. The recollection of breath control. The overseer of the next station is Israfil (peace be upon him). The recollection of this station is breath control, that is, "He" (*Hu*): with

every breath that goes out they say, "O" (*Ya*), and with every breath that goes in, they say, "He" (*Hu*). One practices the recollection, gazing at the membrane of the nose, and one sees this very shape [see figure 11]. Know that the seat is the station of fire. It has a red color, and shadow, and in the middle of three bones there is a red star: it has the influence of the sun [figure 12]. It is at the level of the religious law, and the stage of humanity. The doorway to this station is the two holes in the ears.

FIGURE 11. *Gazing at the nose.*   FIGURE 12. *The red star.*

4. Vocal recollection. The overseer of the next station is 'Azra'il (peace be upon him), and the recollection of this station is the vocal recollection. That is, they recite "the negation and affirmation," "There is no god but God, Muhammad is the Messenger of God." When one performs this recollection with reflection, gazing at the station of the seat, one reflects on that red star. The sign of this station is the spleen.

The composition of the human body. Know that the bodies of the children of Adam have eighteen things. Ten things are from God Most High:

1. spirit
2. breath
3. intellect
4. hearing
5. sight
6. will
7. speech
8. knowledge
9. power
10. character

Four things are from the father:

1. bones
2. skin
3. brain
4. sweat

And four things are from the mother:

1. flesh
2. hair
3. blood
4. fat

The human being is composed of these eighteen things.

Conclusion. Also, at the time of performing recollection, one sits with crossed legs, and grasps the thigh vein of the left leg with the right toe. The recollections are four: the human recollection is vocal, the angelic recollection is breath control, the divine recollection is "the recollection of the mothers," and the Almighty recollection is "the secret and the existence of the Creator."

* * *

ASCENSION THROUGH THE PLANETARY SPHERES

THE THIRD SHATTARI TEXT is a short meditation taken from *The Treasury of Incantations,* composed by Isma'il ibn Mahmud Sindhi Shattari Qadiri of Burhanpur in 1627. He dedicated it to his master 'Isa Jund Allah, whom he had served for twenty years. A dedicated Sufi, he states that he customarily spent nine months each year studying the religious sciences, and three months (Rajab, Sha'ban and Ramadan) in seclusion. He states that he wrote this work while on a long journey that took him to the Punjab and Kashmir, where he conceived the desire to compile this collection of practices while living with dervishes. This text, known in only a single manuscript, is a comprehensive treatise on ritual prayer and meditation, covering required Islamic prayers, divination using the sayings of the Prophet, incantations using the Arabic names of God, non-Arabic divine names, explanations of chants, meditations, and the rules of initiation. The meditation translated here occurs in the midst of the lengthy third chapter on the divine names, and it is of special interest because of the visualization of spiritual ascent through the Heavens, in which the pilgrim is welcomed at each level as a genuine Sufi disciple.

The section begins just after the author has provided a prayer consisting of certain Arabic names of God (omitted in the translation), which lead to the experiences described below when recited a prescribed number of times. Although the author does not explicitly say so, the Nine Lodges seen by the meditating Sufi correspond to the nine planetary Heavens of Islamic cosmology as explained by thinkers like Ibn Sina (Avicenna). The masters presiding over each lodge correspond to the angelic intellects who impart motion to the spheres, and the qualities ascribed to them reflect the characteristics generally assigned to the corresponding planet (I have added these identifications for the reader's convenience). In making this ascension to the divine beyond (which is literally "no-place"), the Sufi is recapitulating the Heavenly journey of the Prophet Muhammad.

The Nine Lodges
ISMA'IL IBN MAHMUD SINDHI SHATTARI

After purifying the soul, cleansing the heart, and illuminating the spirit, one should also enter into the incantation of this name, which is called "the supreme praise." Then one can choose the time of seclusion and recite it the prescribed number of times. The rare and strange properties of the name will become apparent in him. For example, suddenly one night the spirits of the prophets will come in front of him and salute him, performing ritual prayer. He should perform the recitation of the name, standing when they stand and sitting when they sit. After completing the prayer of the spirits, the prophet who is acting as prayer leader (the imam) asks him what he wants. He answers, "It is not concealed from you," and continues to recite the name. When the imam asks again, "What do you want?" he says, "I want to see God and to know the realities of things." The imam says, "Rise, and come with me and perform the recitation of the name, until I bring you by stages to the Nine Lodges and show you its rarities and wonders." Saying nothing, he rises and puts away fear, though many spirits are around him.

The Heaven of the Moon. When they come to the First Lodge, they see a master with a single eye; there is a disturbance taking place in front of him. They salute him. The worshiper should stand at a distance in silence. They will ask the master about his state. The master says, "I have ascertained from the hidden world that this man is accepted."

The Heaven of Mercury. After they move on further, when they reach the Second Lodge, they see a master with the appearance of a Sufi, with several notebooks in front of him. Him too they salute, asking him about the man's state. He replies, "I have read in my book that this man is accepted by the Presence."

The Heaven of Venus. When they reach the Third Lodge, they see a handsome man with musical instruments before him. Him too they salute, asking him about the man's state. He replies, "I have previously learned of the acceptance of this man in the secrets of my melody."

The Heaven of the Sun. When they reach the Fourth Lodge, the universal manifestation of existing things is displayed; the very being of the one practicing the incantation becomes the essence of light, which is a sign of that station. In that place, there is a spiritual person who is characterized by all praiseworthy attributes. Before him there are many swords, and several sweetly singing birds are in flight around his enclosure. Having saluted him, they also ask him about the man's state. He replies, "Before the creation of Adam, I knew that this man was accepted at the divine court."

The Heaven of Mars. When they reach the Fifth Lodge, they see a reddish person with a naked sword in his hand. Him too they salute and ask about the man's state. He replies, "For some years before this, I knew that this man is accepted by the Presence."

The Heaven of Jupiter. When they reach the Sixth Lodge, they see a luminous master in the garb of religious scholars and judges, sitting down. Him too they salute and ask about the man's state. He replies, "In the Hidden Tablet, I have read that this man is accepted at the court."

The Heaven of Saturn. When they reach the Seventh Lodge, they see a master of black color, awe-inspiring and fearsome, with various things in front of him. Him too they salute and ask about the man's state. He replies, "Some years before this, I knew that this man is accepted by the Presence."

The Heaven of the signs of the zodiac. When they reach the Eighth Lodge, they see all that they saw in the lodges before; they see some people standing, some kneeling, some sitting, and some in prostration. Some recite the chant "There is no god but God, Adam is the Pure One of God." Some recite the chant "There is no god but God,

Abraham is the Friend of God." Some recite the chant
"There is no god but God, Ishmael is the Sacrifice of God."
Some recite the chant "There is no god but God, Moses is
the Speaker with God." Some recite the chant "There is no
god but God, Jesus is the Spirit of God." Some recite the
chant "There is no god but God, Muhammad is the Messenger of God." Some perform community prayer, while
others pray alone; some are known as wayfarers and some
are not. Around the lodge, luminous lamps are hung. The
spirits of the prophets salute this group, and they reply,
continuing their prayer. The wayfarer should watch over his
state and follow them. Suddenly the emperor of the prophets rises and shouts, "Servants of God! The pure, the knowers, the upright! Listen, listen, listen!" When he says these
words three times, that clamor and furor of chanting and
murmured prayer falls silent, and the group of spirits becomes still. They listen, and the Prophet delivers a sermon
in praise of the exalted Creator. He says, "What do you
say in regard to the acceptance of this wayfarer?" They all
recognize him.

The Heaven of Heavens, or the Prime Mover. They pass
onward, and when they reach the Ninth Lodge, there they
see a master seated. The spirits of the prophets salute him,
and he replies, saluting them. Our Prophet Muhammad
asks regarding the acceptance of this wayfarer, and he replies, "Some years before this, I saw the acceptance of this
man in the Hidden Tablet." As the master replies, every one
of his hairs begins to speak. The spirits of the prophets ask
more questions about the hidden world where God resides.

He replies, "It is 'no-place,' for only God's emanation goes to a place."

Then this master and the group of prophets begin to offer supplications for the acceptance of this man. Suddenly the divine decree comes forth: "Muhammad! For the love of you, I accept this wayfarer, and I convey him to the rank of the saints."

Then comes the decree, "Return, return!" The spirits of the prophets with the residents of each lodge go back until they enter the room of the wayfarer. After shaking hands with him, they go back. From love of them, and separation from them, a painful disturbance enters the wayfarer's heart.

* * *

PRACTICES OF THE ORDERS

THE SUFI ORDERS were not rigidly exclusive organizations, and in fact there were many cases of multiple initiations, in which Sufis would be trained in the practices of a number of different orders besides the one to which they owed primary allegiance. Manuals of Sufi practice accordingly often list the distinctive meditations of several different orders. Muhammad al-Sanusi (d. 1853) was a North African Sufi who wrote a summary of the practices of forty different Sufi orders into which he had been initiated. In each case, he describes the formula of divine names, or recollection (*dhikr*), that is characteristic of the order. The three examples given here are the Qadiri order, named after 'Abd al-Qadir al-Jilani (d. 1166), which is widely distributed in most

Muslim countries; the Mevlevi order (the "whirling der-vishes"), based in Turkey and associated with the poet Rumi (d. 1273); and the Khawatiri order, founded by 'Ali ibn Maymun al-Idrisi (d. 1511) and located in North Africa. In each case the author focuses on the chanted recollec-tions of God's names and the details of meditative practice associated with them. These instructions include breath control and the manner in which one "strikes the beat" of the chant by concentrating on a particular direction or part of the body. He also provides long lists of the masters in each lineage that he has received, but these have been omitted from the translation.

from *The Clear Fountain*
Muhammad al-Sanusi

The Path of the Qadiri Masters

This path is connected to the master 'Abd al-Qadir al-Jilani (may God sanctify his secret). It is based upon vocal recollection, gathered in the circle, and severe asceticism in seclusion, with gradual reduction of food and avoidance of people. The spiritual path of the Qadiri Masters is asso-ciated at the beginning with summoning the majesty and greatness of God. By this the carnal soul is tamed and edu-cated, because training by the divine majesty helps to purify one more quickly from frivolities.

Their manner of sitting for recollection is that one sits

cross-legged, holding the big toe of the right foot on the vein called *al-kimas*, which is the large vein in the hollow of the left knee joint. One places the hands on the knees, opening up the fingers in the form of the word *Allah*. One recites the L, drawing it out until the heart opens up, and the divine illuminations are unveiled. Then one recites the recollection *awurda barday* [*words unintelligible*], or the recollection of ego annihilation and divine presence attributed to the master of masters, my lord 'Abd al-Qadir. In that, one sits as previously described, turning one's face toward the right shoulder, saying "*ha.*" One then turns the face to the left, saying, "*hu.*" And one bows the head, beating with the breath on the word "*hayy,*" and repeating the practice without interruption.

One of the things for which the people of this cloak are extremely famous comes from the mastery of my lord 'Umar al-'Urabi. He has a useful litany that he recites with the permission of God, adding it to the morning prayer and the prayer between evening and nightfall. I transmit this path from ten different sources, because it has been transmitted to me by my master Abu al-'Abbas al-'Ara'ishi, who had all of these initiations.

The Path of the Mevlevi Masters

This path is based on the constant practice of recollection and following the path of love. They are concerned with achieving breath control, because it is conducive to cutting off satanic insinuations, preventing destructive thoughts, purifying the heart, preserving bodily health, and averting old age, so much so that some of them call it "the water of life." Breathing is a necessary and universal condition engendered by abundant food. If one wishes to become practiced in its control, one should decrease food intake by degrees. One of the characteristics of this group is silent recollection with breath control, and spinning on the heel until one is internally absorbed in the recollected One through periodic witnessing, from internal to external, and from external to internal.

One of the characteristics of the Mevlevi masters is the practice of the recollection "He (*Hu*)" in group assemblies, in which they stand in a circle, each of them placing the palms of the hands on the arms of the person opposite, linking them together. Then, after reciting the Opening (Q 1) and Sincerity (Q 112), they hasten to recite "He (*Hu*)" while they are turning around the pivot point of union with God, until each of them returns to his original starting position. In this way they do seven cycles. Then they stop, and the singer recites appropriate words from the mystical poets. Then they resume the seventh cycle, and so forth, according to their capability. The reciter plays the reed flute to them as they turn in the recollection, and he blows on it so that they proceed to recollection, by reason of the ecstasy that increases from remembering the primordial covenant, and from hearing the words "Am I not your Lord?" (Q 7:172). And when they proceed with that in this fashion, whenever they are overcome by a divine attraction, it shatters the cage of nature. The spirit is released from the disasters of the veils of time, so that it may ascend to the presences of the divine beneficence.

Some of those who are attached to this order practice the recollection of the owl, which is mentioned by the master Jalal al-Din Rumi, as he learned from his master, Shams al-Tabrizi. It is related from him that one day he saw upon the divine throne a bird lowering its head and reciting a recollection. He said, "Then from its recollection I was seized by a longing and a mystical experience, so that I imitated its action and practiced it. The method of it is that one says the syllables *haqqam, haqaqam, haqiqi,* and one imagines the divine names, Merciful, Compassionate, Exalter, striking three beats on the right side. Then one says *baqqam, baqaqam, baqiqi*, and one imagines the divine names Renewer, Source, Extender, striking three beats on the left side. Then one says *haqqam, haqaqam, haqiqi,* and one imagines the divine names Holy, Perfect, Glorious, striking three beats in front. The manner of striking is learned from the master."

One of their characteristics is reading the book of the *Mathnawi* before listening to music. They wear long robes and hats of wool, and they tie turbans with ropes that they call "independence." This alludes to the basis of their path in departure from customary affections, independence from carnal desires, and watching for imaginary thoughts of perfection. They seek God's aid by struggling with the carnal soul through celibacy.

The Path of the Khawatiri Masters

The basis of this path is the recollection of the two phrases of affirming divine unity ("There is no god but

God") in this manner. That is, one sits as one sits for ritual prayer, closes the eyes, and takes hold of the ninety-nine-bead rosary in the right hand, placing it on the left leg, and holding the breath. Then one forcefully draws out the phrase "there is no" from above the navel, with the breath that is between the flanks, raising the head toward the right shoulder, and picturing the word "god" on the shoulder. Then one leaves it for the phrase "but God," placing that on the portion of the heart called "two bow lengths" (Q 53:9), between the breastbones on the right side. One bends the head toward it, repeating that several times, with attention to the meaning of the recollection in the heart: "There is no god but God," i.e., "There is no worshipped one except God." By this one purifies the heart from relying on goods and depending on people. Then one considers the meaning, "There is no goal but God." By it one repels destructive thoughts. Then one considers, "There is no existence but God." By it one negates otherness and ego. Then, "There is nothing witnessed but God." By it one attains witnessing of the divine presence and absorption in the holy illuminations. Another of their characteristics is the practice of discipline and isolation.

4

DIVINE AND HUMAN LOVE

THE SUBJECT of divine love is one that received attention early in the history of the Sufi movement. Emi-
nent mystics of Baghdad, like Rabi'a, Nuri, and Hallaj,
meditated on the verses in the Qur'an which speak of the
mutual love of God and humanity. They identified passionate love ('ishq) as one of the essential qualities of God. Still,
there was inevitably some ambiguity about the relationship
between divine and human love. The delight and tension
that characterize love's ambiguity called forth a series of
remarkable literary productions in Persian on the subject of
divine and human love. Ahmad al-Ghazali (d. 1126) and his
disciple 'Ayn al-Qudat Hamadani (executed 1132) wrote
powerful and evocative interpretations of love (Sawanih,
Tamhidat) that have remained classics of mystical literature. Another outstanding work in this tradition was The
Jasmine of the Lovers by Ruzbihan Baqli (d. 1209), the introductory chapter of which is translated below. Ruzbihan,
who lived in Shiraz in southern Persia, was a prolific author
of mystical texts in Arabic and Persian, including an important Sufi commentary on the Qur'an and a spiritual diary
(which I recently translated under the title The Unveiling

of Secrets). The Jasmine of the Lovers builds on the Arabic tradition of courtly love that developed among the urbane and literate poets and philosophers of the 'Abbasid caliphate. Ruzbihan goes beyond this essentially secular portrait of love, however, by joining it to the growing tradition of Persian poetry and the mystical interpretation of the Qur'an and the sayings of the Prophet Muhammad. Remarkably, the introductory chapter consists largely of a dialogue between Ruzbihan and an unnamed female interlocutor (this is not obvious at first, because Persian lacks grammatical gender, but as the conversation shifts to the higher register of Arabic, it is clear that Ruzbihan's questioner is a woman). Who could she have been? It is possible that this was his favorite wife, whose death threw Ruzbihan into an intense depression, and whom he often saw in his visions of Paradise. Or it could have been a singer with whom Ruzbihan fell in love while on pilgrimage to Mecca, an experience that caused him to abandon temporarily his position as a Sufi master. In any case, Ruzbihan sets the stage for this dialogueue by recounting a mystical experience in which he is ravished of all created qualities and transported into the divine presence. God informs Ruzbihan that he will be tested in love, and this test takes the form of a delightful interrogation by the unnamed woman, whose beauty threatens to overwhelm him. She demands that Ruzbihan explain the relation between divine and human love, with justification from the Qur'an and the Prophet. She enraptures Ruzbihan in love, even as she stands revealed as the human manifestation of the divine qualities of beauty and majesty. As the dialogue concludes, she is so impressed by Ruzbihan's answers that she asks him to compose a complete treatise in Persian on mystical love, which he agrees to do; he has passed the test. The complete translation of this challenging and elusive book is a task for the future.

On the Courtesy of the Lover and Beloved
RUZBIHAN BAQLI

. . . You must understand, my brother (may God bless your understanding and the time of your love), that when I arrived from the journey of servanthood to the world of lordship, and I saw the beauty of the angelic world with the angelic eye, I traveled through the way stations of unveilings, and I ate the meal of spiritual stations and miracles at the table of spiritual beings. With the birds of the Throne I flew through the atmosphere of 'Illiyin (the Highest Heaven), and I beheld the pure manifestation of the witnessing of God (great is His name) with His single eye. The wine of His majestic love reached the taste of my soul in the cup of pure beauty. The sweetness of eternal love cloaked my heart with the garment of divine knowledge and primordial unveilings.

In the ocean of divine knowledge I became strengthened by God, and on its surges in the ship of wisdom I cut through the waves of grace and wrath, and I reached the shores of the divine attributes and actions. By degrees I went through the knowledge of unity, isolation, and detachment toward the world of pre-eternity, and I found the clothing of eternity. I heard the speech of greatness, might, beauty, and nearness. The annihilation of unity showed its power to me, and it annihilated me from all the traces of time in the essence of eternity. It made me eternally present.

God took me to His own sanctuary, and He removed the cloak of servanthood from me. He cloaked me with the clothing of freedom, and He said, "You have become a passionate lover, a tender lover, a pure lover, one who longs, one who is free, one who speaks ecstatically, one who is comely, one who is united, one who is sincere. So create by My creation, look by My glance, hear by My hearing, speak by My tongue, judge by My wisdom, and love by My love. In truth, you are one of My saints. You are in My immaculate sanctuary, and by the essence of My grace I have made you safe from My wrath. But I will test you with the sufferings of love, and I will examine your truth. I will save anyone who loves you from the pain of My punishment, for he will be among the chosen disciples of My lovers."

When my soul attained the time of the angelic realm and the day of the realm of power, pain appeared in me, and I saw myself perplexed in the trial of love. When I came out again from that world, in these conditions of testing I became afflicted both by finding love and by not finding it. Then I sat down in the world of beauty. My spirit was wounded by the arrows of love in the way-station of trial. My carnal soul sought for physical sweetness, while my intellect looked for eternity in the beauty of the Creator. Suddenly, in the burning of that melancholy love of God's beauty, I traveled to the world of time. My fate was to come to the marketplace of beauty, and in every shell I sought for a pearl of grace. Suddenly, in the plaza of generosity, I saw the beauty of those attributes in the mirror of divine signs.

The bird in the garden of pre-eternity had been hidden in the nest of divine actions by the veil of creation. The clothing of "We created man in the most beautiful of stations" (Q 95:4) was adorned with the beauty of "He has made your forms beautiful" (Q 40: 66), with the beautiful meaning of "God created Adam in His own form." The creativity of the Creator was lost in the creature. I knew what a rarity this was, and what it was. Irresistibly the eye of my soul remained in that mirror of divine signs, and the turbulence of love overpowered me. The eye of the soul remained upon the Creator, while the eye of the intellect remained in creation, because of its infidelity. With the eye of the spirit, I saw the beauty of eternity, and with the eye of the intellect I had the power to understand the form of Adam.

She said to me, "Look with the human eye upon the human world." The eye of the heart joined the eye of physical forms, and I saw her, a fairy creature whose loveliness and beauty made all creatures of the world fall in love. She appeared so disbelieving, tricky, deceitful, forward, and roguish, that a hundred thousand angels fell at a blink of her eye, and a thousand armies of the devil were present in a single curl of her tress. The color of her complexion put

Venus to shame, and in Heaven she boasted to Jupiter of her loveliness and beauty.

The deer of her love strode proudly forth to hunt lions. With gracefulness she drove wild the ascetics from the monasteries of the angelic realm. I looked upon this from the path of pride, and by way of self-denial I seized the veil of modesty. With a pearly tongue I said to her:

> You are higher than substance and accident,
>   you are the goal of the whole creation.
> Your throne and carpet are the royal court,
>   creation is nothing but your workshop.

What a bold vision this is! In Sufism, to look upon something other than God is infidelity, and to look upon intellect and knowledge destroys life!

Out of extreme happiness I told her, "You are a member of the company of lovers who know God, you beauty! For you are fully worthy, even if you do not drink the wine of love with me in the assembly of selflessness." She said to me, "To come back from that world is heedlessness, and to gaze at me is the occasion for disaster; perhaps you have lost the way." I said, "There are many who lose the way in love. Intellect is unable to attain your love and still remain in that divine love. Tell me, who are you? Are you in God's essence, or could you be in the secret of God's actions in the world?" She said, "The secret of divinity is unaffected by incarnation in humanity. But the beauty of humanity is from the reflection of divine beauty. The beginning of creation is mine, but the end of the affair belongs to God."

> I said, "You whose beauty is my very soul,
>   won't you tell me where you're from?"
> She said, "I was fashioned by divinity,
>   I am the guide and leader of humanity.
> "I am the first creation in the world,
>   and I display my face everywhere.
> "I do little with the base and lowly;
>   my nature is far removed from creatures.
> "God looks on me from all creation,
>   yet my creation's separate from all creation."

She said, "You fool, again! Do you play the fool with me again? Anyone who gets accustomed to me takes on the color of the original source of beauty from the pure soul of souls, and no longer retains the slightest shade of time. The spirit of the world of worlds is annihilated in the soul of anyone who shares my color."

> Whatever has a place upon God's porch
> has a soul that also descends to brick and stone.

I saw the secret of beauty in the majesty of nature's loveliness, as the portrait of that bridal rose. The pre-eternal light of her ruby lips pulled the holy spirits[1] into the source of love's annihilation with the lasso of fate. It was laughter that appeared on the lips of the holy spirit, and its spiritual companions, like the universal intellect and universal soul,

---

[1] In Islamic tradition the concept of "holy spirit" is not associated with the Christian doctrine of the Trinity but is broadly associated with the highest angels (such as Gabriel) and the inspiration of the prophets.

found their souls bewildered in the hand of fate, in that soul of souls.

> From the power of that laughing lip,
> Fate was stunned, with a finger resting on his teeth.

When I looked well, I saw the purity of her soul's attributes in a form that had no place. The essence of reality was in the human form, but it left no trace. The place that I call the city of God is the place of the soul, but it does not contain the soul. In happiness she opened up the palace and beheld me, a foolish lover. Quickly and elegantly, she was about to turn her head away from me. I said, "The reflection of your spirit is united with God's spirit, you are the purity of the outward form of things, the shade of the wall of the Ka'ba of power, and the shadow of my soul. What then is this ill temper? When love's affair has come to this end, to turn away from me is the action of the immature." She said, "What are you saying? The words of love are subtle, and if they are not found, the work of love becomes tired of love. Even if this does not bore you, I have things to do." The effect this had on me is alluded to in the following verse:

> If for a single moment I could tell you of my sorrow,
> My whole life would not be worth that single moment.

She said, "I have seen that Sufism is not the path of licentiousness, and gazing upon me is not the job of saints. The penetrating gaze of meditation is on the limited creation, but the wise ones of reality have their powerful gaze on the beauty of Almighty Power in the beauty of the created image. The carnal soul has no real delight in this limited world, for whoever treats the carnal soul as a guide is no real man in the divine knowledge of reality. Look with the eye of the Truth, if you are looking at a creation in which there is a Renewer and a Creator, and look with the Truth at the Almighty Power there."

After all that, she tested me, saying, "Sufi! What does this worldly love have to do with that divine love?" I said, "Your worldly love is the beginning of that divine love. For both beginner and adept there is an unavoidable condition for reaching the intoxication of divine love—and that is to clothe the created with divinity." She said, "Perhaps my love is a mistake in your path." I said, "There is proof in support of chaste love in the religious law of Muhammad (God's prayers be upon him)." She said, "What is the proof?" I said, "The word of God (who is great and mighty): 'We shall tell you the most beautiful of stories' (Q 12:3), that is, we shall tell you the story of the lover and the beloved, Joseph and Zulaykha (peace be upon them), and also the love of Jacob and Joseph (peace be upon them), for the tale of love is the most beautiful of stories for those who have passion and love.

"And there is the word of the Prophet (peace be upon him), 'One who loves, is chaste, loves in secret, and then dies, dies as a martyr.' And he also said (peace be upon him), 'One who is overwhelmed with love by God, for God, and in God, loves the beautiful face.' Dhu al-Nun said (God have mercy on him), 'One who is intimate with God is intimate with every lovely thing and glorious face.' He also said, 'The one who is intimate with God is intimate with every lovely thing and with all beautiful forms.' In these matters, the people of divine knowledge have secrets that cannot rightly be unveiled except to those who are worthy of them. One who spills them before the unworthy has earned punishment and difficulties."

After these proofs, she told me, "You are fairly clever in this science. Is it absolutely permissible to love God Most High passionately? And is it permissible for someone to claim His love? And is the name of love one of the names that applies both to God and humanity among the lovers? Is there permission for love for God, from God, in God, and by God?" I said, "Our masters differ about that. Among them there are those who deny it, and among them there are those who declare it to be permissible. And the ones who deny it are merely concealing this secret from the people of this world out of jealousy toward the people, while the ones who declare it permissible do so from their boldness in love and expansiveness. And the lovers and beloveds 'do not fear the blame of a blamer' because of God, 'which is the grace that God gives to those whom he wills, for God is the Comprehender, the Knower' (Q 5:54).

"Those who declare that love is permissible include 'Abd al-Wahid ibn Zayd and the people of Damascus, Abu Yazid al-Bistami, Abu al-Qasim Junayd, Abu al-Husayn al-Nuri, Dhu al-Nun al-Misri, Yusuf ibn al-Husayn al-Razi, Abu Bakr al-Wasiti, al-Husri, al-Husayn ibn Mansur al-Hallaj, and Shibli. And our master and leader Abu 'Abd Allah Muhammad ibn Khafif (God have mercy on him) used to deny love at first, until the question of love was raised with him by Abu al-Qasim Junayd. At that time he discussed the meaning of love, the derivation of its name, and how Abu

'Abd Allah distinguished it and what he said about it. So he turned away from his denial, and he declared love permissible and composed an opinion concerning it.

"It is transmitted from the Prophet (may God bless him and grant him peace) that God Most High said, 'When I know that absorption in Me dominates the heart of My servant, I make My servant long for intimate conversations with Me. And when My servant is like that, and My servant is going to neglect Me, I place between him and his negligence of Me those who are My friends in truth (i.e., the saints), those who are the heroes, the ones for whose sake I turn away My gaze from the people of the earth when I wish to punish them.'

"It is related that David (peace be upon him) used to be called the lover of God. And the people of the tribe of Quraysh said, 'Muhammad is in love with his Lord.' These are proofs of the permissibility of the love of God (who is great and mighty)—or rather, they prove that the Prophet is the love of the lordly ones, the substance of the love of the spiritual ones, the gift of the Truth to humanity, which descended from the oceans of mercy, and issued from the sources of divine knowledge, as the beloved of Adam and the goal of the world and of Adam, the pure and passionate lover of God, Muhammad the chosen one (prayers of God be upon him).

"Now, it is known that the loves of Layli and Majnun, Jamil and Buthayna, Da'd and Rabab, Wamiq and 'Adhra, Hind and Bishr, and their likes and peers among Arabs and Persians, are famous among the intellectuals and the learned. The wise ones of reality know that affection is beyond the reproach of nature. The philosopher sages have said that chaste love is the affection of spirits and the patience of bodies. Some of the emperors of divine knowledge, when they were beginners, have also found their holy birds fallen into the cage of human love, like Abu al-Husayn al-Nuri, Abu al-Gharib al-Isfahani, and Bishr and Hind among the companions of the Prophet. The pearl of the ocean of their love was transferred from the world of trial to the world of love. Muhammad, the prince of the horizons, was aware of their condition, and he had mercy upon them and said, 'Praise be to God, who placed among my people the likes of Joseph and Zulaykha.'

"And also on the subject of human love, which is the path to divine love, consider what God has said on this subject: 'Fear God, for you are hiding in your soul that which God brought about' (Q 33:37, the Prophet's love for Zaynab); 'this brother of mine has ninety-nine sheep, and I have a single sheep' (Q 38:23, the parable of David's love for Bathsheba); 'she desired him, and he desired her' (Q 12:24, Joseph and Zulaykha). Read from the Book about the prophets, so that you will know that in love this worldly gaze is not there. In that divine love, we have no way of crossing the flood of divine unity without the bridge of your worldly love. The prophets and saints are sanctified beyond the reproach of natural lusts in human love. This is a point known only to those who have experienced being clothed with divinity in love."

When she saw me speaking in terms of philosophy and religious law, eloquent in both languages, she said, "Sufi and knower of God! I see that you are an ocean in divine knowledge and a scholar in philosophy. I love your graceful goodness and the freshness of your magnanimity and your beauty. By God! Are you able to explain to me human love in relation to divine love, in the Persian language, in a short book, so that it would be the guide for us and for all lovers and beloveds, and the destination for the lovers who are on the path?"

I said, "At your command! I shall commence it, completing my promise to you well and fulfilling your command for love of you. For the lover is commanded by the beloved, and one who longs belongs to the object of longing; he does what he is asked.

> If your love is true, I will obey it,
> for the lover is obedient to the one he loves."

So I wrote a book explaining human love and divine love, with the aid of God and His wonderful assistance, so that it would be the delight of intimacy and the fragrance of the secret enclosure, and I called it *The Jasmine of the Lovers*, arranging it in thirty-one chapters.

5

LISTENING TO MUSIC

L ISTENING TO MUSIC has been a controversial practice
in the Islamic tradition, partly because instrumental
music was not a developed art form in the culture of Arabia
during the lifetime of the Prophet Muhammad. And in addition, music was associated with courtly lifestyles and with
nonreligious and immoral behavior. Nevertheless, there
was an undeniable musical effect in listening to the recitation of the Qur'an, which enhanced receptivity to the divine
word through the melodious medium of the human voice.
From the earliest times, Sufis found that listening to recited
poetry, particularly when it contained the imagery of love
and intoxication, was one of the best ways to enhance spiritual ecstasy and higher states of consciousness. But in
order to insure that listening to music was associated with
spiritual development rather than the satisfaction of selfish
desire, it was necessary to set forth strict criteria for the
proper way to listen to music. Most of the standard handbooks of Sufi practice have a detailed section explaining the
principles and practices of listening to music.

One such discussion comes from the seventh chapter of
The Treatise on Holiness, a manual of Sufism written by

Ruzbihan Baqli (see biographical note on page 82). This is a work addressed to Sufi novices, which also discusses the divine unity, knowledge of God, spiritual states and practices, and the psychology of mystical experiences. Rather than describing the outward details of listening to music, the text deals instead with its cosmic and psychological aspects, based upon the different levels and types of spiritual aspirants. Ruzbihan expresses this in his characteristically dense poetic images, at the same time linking his spiritual insights firmly to the examples of the prophets and saints of the past. Ruzbihan cites the sayings "I am the Truth" and "Glory be to Me," two famous ecstatic utterances associated with the early Sufi masters Hallaj and Abu Yazid al-Bistami. Although it would appear that the speakers were claiming to be God, Sufi interpreters maintain that the egos of these saints had been annihilated, so that it was in fact the voice of God speaking through them. Music brings about many such paradoxes.

Ruzbihan also cites an important Qur'anic text that the Sufis understand in terms of music. "Am I not your Lord?" (Q 7:172) was the question addressed by God to the unborn souls of humanity, in the pre-eternal time before the world was created. When those human souls answered, "Yes," they sealed the primordial covenant with God for all time. According to the standard Sufi interpretation, the love of music is based upon the faint recollection of hearing the beautiful voice of God saying, "Am I not your Lord?" Listening to music therefore becomes a way of transporting oneself back to that moment of harmony with God in pre-eternity.

On Listening to Music
Ruzbihan Baqli

Know, my brothers (may God increase the delight of your life in listening to music) that the principles of listening to music are according to the types of lovers of God. There is a beginning and an end to it. The enjoyment of spirits in music varies; the holy ones find enjoyment from that music in accordance with their spiritual station. But only those who are authorities in mystical knowledge are prepared for it, because in music spiritual attributes are mixed with bodily natures; as long as the dirt is not cleaned off, one does not become a listener in the assemblies of intimacy. Yes, all of existing things, whatever living things there are, yearn to listen to music, because each one has a particular spiritual capacity of its own; it lives by that spirit. And that spirit lives by listening to music.

Listening to music is the refreshment of all thoughts from the weight of humanity. It is the agitator of human natures and the mover of divine secrets. For some it is a temptation, since they are imperfect, but for others it is a sign, since they are perfect. Those whose physical natures are living, but whose hearts are dead, should not listen to music, because it bears harmful fruit for them. One whose heart is cheerful, regardless of whether he has reached the Beloved or not, should be listening to music. In music there are a hundred thousand pleasures, and with a single one of those pleasures, one can travel the path of mystical knowledge for a thousand years; this feat would not be easy, even for a knower of God, on the basis of religious devotion alone.

The one who seeks to listen to music should have veins that are purified of base desires and filled with light from purity of devotion. He should be present and listening in the divine presence with his very soul, in order to be far from the temptation of the carnal soul in listening to music—and this is not guaranteed except for those who are strong in love. For listening to music is God's listening to music; it is from God, by God, in God, and with God. If one makes any of these relationships with something other than God, he is an infidel, he has lost the way, and he has not drunk the wine of union while listening to music.

The disciples of love listen without the carnal soul, the travelers of longing listen to music without the intellect, those who are bewildered by love listen to music without the heart, and those who are astounded by intimacy listen to music without the spirit. If they listen with any of these faculties, they are veiled from God. If they listen with the carnal soul, they become heretics; if they listen with the intellect, they become interpreters; if they listen with the heart, they become observers; and if they listen with the spirit, they become present—and listening to music is beyond presence. It is wonderment and raving, astonishment upon astonishment. In that world, conventions are cut off, the world is ignorant, and the lover is annihilated.

The listener and the reciter are one at the feast of love. The reality of the lovers' path is listening to music, but the reality of its reality is without listening. Listening comes from the speech of God, and the absence of listening goes with contemplation of divine beauty. When there is language, there is distance, but when there is silence, there is nearness. When there is hearing, there is ignorance, and the ignorant ones are in duality. In listening to music, wisdom is isolated, the commandment is forbidden, and the negation is itself negated. In the beginning of listening to music, all negations were negated, and all negated things became negations.

Listening to music is the key to the treasure of realities, and it is apportioned to the knowers of God in different ways. Some listen with spiritual stations, some listen with spiritual states, some listen with unveilings, and some listen with witnessings. When they are in spiritual stations, they are in trouble; when they are in spiritual states, they are at their source; when they are in unveiling, they are in union; and when they are in witnessing, they are in beauty.

From the beginning of spiritual stations to their end, there are one hundred thousand stations, in each of which there are a million kinds of listening to music. In each kind of listening to music, a million qualities enter, such as transformation and reproach, separation and union, nearness and distance, burning and agitation, hunger and thirst, fear and hope, warning and sighs, raving and wonderment, purity and chastity, servanthood and lordship. If even one of these qualities reached the souls of all the ascetics of the world, their souls would spontaneously leave them.

In the same way, from the first beginning of the spiritual states to their end, there are a million stations, in each of which there are a thousand hints in listening to music. And in every hint there are different kinds of pain, such as love and longing, passion and burning, exclusivity, craving, and fortune. If even one of them passed through the hearts of all disciples, their heads would break off from their bodies.

Likewise, from the first unveiling to the last, in listening to music there is apparition upon apparition. If all the lovers saw even one of these apparitions, they would melt like quicksilver. Likewise, in witnessing, a hundred thousand qualities enter a hundred times during listening to music. Each one of these prepares a thousand graces in the knower of God, such as divine knowledge and reality, penetrations and lightning flashes, lights of holiness and awe, stability and rapture, constriction and expansiveness, ability, and quietude. It casts him into the hidden of the hidden, and it displays to him marvelous secrets.

From every leaf in the Paradise of witnessing, on the trees of the attributes, the birds of light recite an endless song with the chanting of eternity before their hearts' beloved. One word of that song annihilates the knower of God from his condition of servanthood, and he subsists in the Godhood. He takes his character from God, and gives his own character away. He is familiar with himself and estranged from himself, he knows by himself and is bold by himself. He makes himself afraid of himself, and in the state of essential union he manifests himself in his own color. He speaks of the hidden of the hidden with God, and he listens to the speech of love from the tongue of his pain.

Sometimes God says, "You are Me," and sometimes he says, "I am you." Sometimes God makes him subsist in annihilation, and sometimes He annihilates him in subsistence. Sometimes God pulls him, and sometimes He gives him rest in intimacy. Sometimes God wounds him with the arrows of unity, and sometimes He makes his soul live by clothing it in divinity. Sometimes God listens, sometimes He quotes, and sometimes He recites. Sometimes God casts him into pure servanthood, and sometimes He casts him into the essence of lordship. Sometimes God intoxicates him with beauty, and sometimes He abases him with majesty. Sometimes God brings him to the desert, sometimes He gives him stability, and sometimes He gives him rapture. Sometimes God seizes his soul with the religion of music, and sometimes He seats him in royal authority on the celestial vault of divine greatness, with the penetrating grip of the endless light of the dawnings of unity. Sometimes God lets him fly in the air of pre-eternity with the secret of holiness, and sometimes He clips the wings of concentration with the scissors of transcendence in the atmosphere of His identity.

All these things and much more than this are found in listening to music. There is one person who knows this: in the essence of witnessing, in the witnessing of beauty, and in the presence of the Presence, he takes the wine of affection from the Eternal Cupbearer who is unaffected by nonexistence. He listens to the word of the morning in the dawn of holiness in the hidden things of the spirit. That person who is there knows, but here no one knows the explanation of that.

This word is not for the immature, since they conceive of God in human terms, nor is this information for those who are estranged, since they deprive God of all qualities. This is the heritage of Moses, the cipher of Jesus, the burn-

ing of Adam, the friendship of Abraham, the weeping of
Jacob, the pain of Isaac, the stability of Ishmael, the singing
of David, the fellowship of Noah, the flight of Jonah, the
chastity of Joseph, the suffering of Job, the healing of John
the Baptist, the fear of Zachariah, the longing of Jethro, and
the witnessing and unveiling of the beloved Muhammad
(the prayers of the merciful God be upon them all).

This tale is the secret of Hallaj's saying, "I am the Truth,"
and the reality of the word of Bayazid, "Glory be to Me!"
Sari Saqati had the reality of listening to music, Abu Bakr
Wasiti had the language of listening to music, and Shibli
had the pain of listening to music. Listening to music is
permitted to the lovers, but it is forbidden to the common
people.

Listening to music is of three kinds: there is one kind
for the common people, one kind for the elite, and one kind
for the elite of the elite. The common people listen with
their physical nature, which is begging. The elite listen with
the heart, which is seeking. The elite of the elite listen with
the soul, which is loving. If I explain listening to music, I
fear that in the world receptive ears will be closed, because
I come from the taverns of annihilation, and I bring the
secret of divine presence. If I speak, I speak without foundation, for if I speak from a foundation, I will speak in
accordance with that foundation. My musician is God, and
I speak from Him; my witness is God, and I see Him; and
my word is the song of the nightingale of "Am I not your
Lord?" (Q 7:172), and I speak to the birds in the nest of pre-
eternity.

My state was strange to every stranger,
And I became a wonder to every wonder.

May God nourish me and you with the nobility of those
who listen to music!

* * *

THE PRACTICES OF LISTENING TO MUSIC

AS A COMPLEMENT to Ruzbihan's cosmic and poetic meditations on music, it is useful to consider a more practical
and performance-based account of listening to music.
Throughout the Indian subcontinent, the tradition of Sufi
music known as *qawwali* has attained immense popularity
through concert performances and recordings, in addition
to the devotional performances that are still held at the
tombs of Sufi saints. Although Sufi handbooks gave considerable emphasis to those who listen to music, very little
attention was actually paid to the performers or musicians,
who (in India, at least) were generally from hereditary low-
caste service guilds. The musicians were there to assist the
spiritual practice of others; their own role was given
scarcely a thought. It is therefore striking to find detailed
consideration of the social and religious role of musicians,
as well as listeners, in a modern discussion of listening to
music written as an appendix to an anthology of Sufi poetry.

The text in question, *The Melodies of Listening to Music*,
was published in Pakistan in 1972 as a kind of chapbook for
the use of *qawwali* performers. A collection of over 200
Persian poems considered basic to the repertoire of *qawwali*

singers, it was based on an earlier anthology published in northern India (Badaon) in 1935. An appendix to the new text, written in Urdu, gives an account of the proper manners for listening to music, and the blessings and dangers that may be associated with this practice. Those who have attended these sessions will recognize the importance of proper external behavior, including one's physical posture; Europeans and Americans unaccustomed to sitting on the floor for long periods of time are definitely at a disadvantage, since informal postures (including sitting cross-legged) are considered insufficiently respectful. The text also provides a defense of music as something that is approved and beneficial according to Islamic norms.

Thus far the book's discussion is quite similar to the treatments of music in classical Sufi handbooks written in previous centuries. There are frequent quotations from early Sufis and from famous Indian Sufi masters (particularly from the Chishti order), and the emphasis is on sincerity and the avoidance of hypocritical display. The author also retains the classical distinction between two kinds of love, worldly or "metaphorical" love on the one hand, and spiritual or real love on the other. The concluding two sections, however, are novel, and the author realizes that this is the case. Here many of his comments are addressed to the economic aspect of musical performance: he urges the singer to avoid haggling over money prior to the performance, after the fashion of the courtesans and other musicians who performed for upper-class patrons. At the same time, he is harsh with listeners who refuse to pay the going rates for the musicians who provide them with spiritual benefits. The author also reiterates the classical emphasis on the importance of words over music, and he briefly mentions the proper ritual method of presenting donations for the singers, preferably through a senior Sufi who is functioning as the master of the assembly.

from *The Melodies of Listening to Music* (1972)

The Practices of Listening to Music

> Come out from the two worlds, when you would enter music.
> Music belongs to you, and you also belong to music.

The revered Junayd of Baghdad (God have mercy on him) said, "In listening to music, think of three things. First is the time." The listener must have complete quietude. Leaving aside all worldly recollections and attachments, collecting his concentration into one center, and abandoning needs and wants, his whole body becomes tasting and longing, and he participates in listening to music. This should not be at the time of ritual prayer and devotions. No worldly need should prevent one's attention and peace of heart. I would also add that it should not be at a time when prostration is forbidden, that is, at the time of sunrise and sunset.

"Second is place." It should not be in a public thoroughfare, but in a remote place protected from noise and confusion. It should be a neat and clean place, with no bad smells to disturb the brain.

"Third is the people." There should be no critics of listening to music, arrogant and dry ascetics, or mannerless people. There should be no fake or hypocritical Sufis. The reflection of the bad thoughts of those people will have an effect on others. The presence of a critic of listening to music is the occasion for troubling thoughts, for it is this very picture of arrogance whose gaze and presence exerts a negative influence. The fake and hypocritical Sufi, by his pretense of ecstasy and dancing, disturbs those who are present. From his fake dance and ecstasy, their spiritual state and grace suffer interruption. In addition to these manners, there are certain other manners that one should keep in mind.

1. One should sit in the assembly having performed ablutions and applied perfume.

2. At the beginning and the end of listening to music, one should recite verses from the Qur'an and the adoration of the Prophet. The revered Mumshad 'Alu Dinawari (d. 911) said, "One day I saw the noble Prophet (may God bless him and grant him peace) in a dream, and I said, 'Messenger of God, do you consider listening to music to be bad?' His grace said, 'I don't consider anything about it to be bad, but I will say to the listeners, that the beginning and end of listening to music should be done with the Qur'an.' "

3. Sit properly. At the time of sitting and rising, bad manners should not be in evidence anywhere, for example, sitting cross-legged, stretching out the feet, or sitting by leaning on something. One should sit on both knees in

complete silence. One should not make any movement that would bother the members of the assembly or disturb their concentration.

4. Keep one's eyes on the face of the master, in order to be protected from making a slip.

5. As far as possible, keep one's temperament settled and quiet. Do not let the divine attractions become disturbing or exciting. Do not let your heart escape your will and control. Do not intentionally seek ecstasy with the thought that people will say, "This person is very hard-hearted, since listening to music has no influence on him." Of course, when it is beyond control, it is by compulsion.

6. It is necessary to follow the people of the assembly in standing. When those who are present stand up because of ecstasy, or in order to display ecstasy, then it is necessary to stand in conformity with them. On one occasion in a certain assembly of listening to music, the revered "emperor of the masters" Nizam al-Din Awliya' (d. 1325) arrived a little late, so he stood in another enclosure. The people of the assembly listening to the music stood up, and so the emperor of the masters also stood up. People said, "Between Your Grace and them there is a considerable distance; you should come here." He said, "It is necessary to be in conformity with the assembly." From this tradition it appears that, if one reaches the assembly late, one should sit wherever one happens to be and avoid disturbing the experience for others. See that this same order and behavior is followed in the assembly.

7. Poetry is generally performed with worldly metaphors, but the interpretation of spiritual reality is also found

in these metaphorical expressions. Therefore, one should not interpret the contents of poetry in terms of the worldly beloved. Rather, every word and melody should be understood as a reality in accordance with the real Beloved. Everything that issues from the breath should be referred to a single essence—moving from traditional expressions to spiritual meanings, from the voice to spirituality, from song to archetypes. For the wayfarer, it is necessary to be free from the literal compositions and to move in the direction of spiritual meanings and understandings. Holding words as really nothing more than a form of dress, one should realize that spiritual meanings and understandings are the essential goal. The revered emperor of the masters is reported to have said, "On Resurrection Day, a divine decree will reach the Sufis and those who listen to music: 'Have you referred the verses you have heard to our qualities?' Those people will say, 'Yes, we have done so.' The guidance of the Most High Creator will be, 'All qualities are temporal, and Our Essence is eternal; therefore how can it be permissible to refer temporal qualities to the Eternal?' They will say, 'Lord, we have done so from extreme love.' His reply will be, 'Since you have done so for love, We have forgiven you, and We have caused Our mercy to rain down upon you.'"

8. Avoid considering the heart-ravishing and enchanting quality of the voice, or the downy cheek and mole of the singer; rather, imagine that God is listening to God.

9. If your temperament is constricted, and you do not fall in love with the singing, then pray for forgiveness; your temperament is not so inclined. It is necessary to leave the

assembly in order to disturb them no more. "The cold heart makes the company cold." Other people present should not insist that such a person should go.

10. If anyone experiences a spiritual state, he should be looked after in such a way that none of his limbs breaks the religious law, and no physical harm reaches him. The master seizes the hand of the person in ecstasy and must not let him out of his grasp. Without such restraint, one frequently suffers constricted or even destructive thoughts. On the release of the person from ecstasy, he should not be disturbed or confined.

The Blessings of Listening to Music

> Music is the bringer of joy and happiness.
> Music is the giver of clarity and light.

The blessings of listening to music are so many that it is completely beyond the ability of this incapable author to mention and enumerate them, but by gathering them into one place, I will state some of these blessings.

1. The revered Junayd of Baghdad (God have mercy on him) said, "There are three times when divine mercy descends upon the Sufis. One is the time of eating food, for the Sufi does not eat without hunger. The second is the time of recollecting God together, for the Sufi does not recollect anything else, except for the stations of the sincere ones. The third is the time of listening to music, for they listen to it with ecstasy, and they are in the presence of God."

2. The origin and source of all ecstasy and happiness that is attained while listening to music is the mercy of God.

3. Just as striking two pieces of iron together produces a spark, in the same way, at the time of listening to music, a light appears, which is related to the world of spirits.

4. While listening to music, when concentration on the world of spirits becomes more perfect, and the heart becomes one-pointed, for this reason at certain times the listener is honored by the good fortune of unveiling.

5. Performing music is itself a cause of happiness and joy. It removes constriction of the heart. Music has a special connection to the spirit.

6. In the unfolding of spiritual stations, only by listening to music can one attain results. Those stations of the spiritual path that one can only reach with difficulty through severe discipline can easily be attained by means of listening to music.

7. When a dervish claps his hands while listening to music, the desire of the hand falls away. If the master claps, then the desire of the master falls away. And when the cry is raised, internal desire moves away.

8. When the divine attractions of love blaze up from listening to music, the fire of love is inflamed. Gentleness appears in the heart.

The Dangers of Listening to Music

> Like the soul, music is near the lords of virtue,
> But it is very far from the corrupt.

First of all, I have said that the influences of things change according to the conditions and circumstances. If contrary principles and rules have a share in listening to music, there will be a powerful burden of harm instead of benefit. Therefore it is necessary to explain certain dangers, so that the people who listen to music may do so carefully and be preserved from harm.

1. The revered Abu 'Umar said, "To show off and display in music—that is, to manifest states that one does not have—is worse than thirty years of error."

2. Whoever dances, moves, and rends clothing while listening to music, with the intention of hypocritically showing himself off in this way as a dervish, will suffer harm. This action of his is completely forbidden, even pointing at it with a finger is forbidden—and that finger is deserving of Hell.

3. After the dissipation of spiritual states and ecstasy, silence and stillness are required. If someone takes the trouble to reveal his previous state of ecstasy and trance, imagining that people will say that it was a wonderful state to have disappeared so quickly, this also enters into error and hypocrisy. One should not allow space in the heart for such impermissible fancies.

4. Listening to music is harmful and even forbidden for someone who is attached to metaphorical love, who says that he is a prisoner of lustful desires and is overpowered by carnal attractions. He will refer the contents of poetry to his own metaphorical beloved, become inflamed with lustful attractions, and will experience immorality and wickedness, which is sin. This worthless one says that if

anyone speaks of metaphorical love as a love in which one is torn to pieces by carnal desires for a youth or a woman, that is an insult to love. This is no kind of love; rather, it is grain rot, satanic power, and psychic confusion.

> Every old goat practices the worship of beauty,
> and now becomes the ornament of wise men's craft.

It is true that it is very difficult to distinguish the difference between the confusion of desire and spiritual love. Spiritual lovers are rarities in existence. Those people are astonishing who, suffering in carnal desires, think that immorality and desire are true love. How well someone has said that beauty and loveliness are for seeing, not for touching.

If someone has love for a youth or woman, and he classifies it under "God is beautiful and loves beauty," he is comparing the beauty and loveliness of the created with the beauty, loveliness, and power of the Creator. The former is called metaphorical love, while the latter falls under the saying "The metaphorical is the bridge to reality."

The Manners of the Musician

> Sweet-voiced musician, sing something fresh and new;
> Look for a wine that makes the heart fresh and new.

Where there are explicit manners for listeners, there also are manners for the speakers. In the time of the classical writings, the manners of the singer were not separately treated, but here and there passing references were made to the singers. From this it appears that in that time, there was no such necessity for rules applying to singers. The singers were generally learned, spiritually sensitive, and stylistically expert, and they passed their time in association with pure and outstanding personalities, a single glance from whom could turn someone into a real human being. It is no wonder that in the beginning the Sufi singer was just a singer, and later on that same singer became the cause of the spiritual advancement in the Sufis. All authoritative opinion agrees that one cannot be a singer without being in the company of Sufis. But since at the present time, the singer is generally illiterate and is excluded from the company of pure souls, therefore I will mention a number of necessary manners for singers. I hope that singers will try to benefit from this.

1. The singer should not be greedy. When the singer is reciting, he should be able to proceed without calculation. Whatever he receives he should regard as a blessing, and accept cheerfully, and no performance of his should cause aversion or distaste. Nor should one first of all settle on the amount of payment, in the style of courtesans. This is highly objectionable, and it is in conflict with the honor of the singer. This is the custom of courtesans and low-caste musical performers, that they set the price for performing or singing, not even setting foot outside their house until the payment is made. But if the singer is invited out, it is no problem if he asks for travel expenses, rather it is the duty of the one who invites him to send adequate travel expenses in advance.

2. The singer should not engage in questionable things.

His habits and character should be good, and he should be bound by the rules of fasting and ritual prayer. While singing he sits in a state of ritual purity, dressed in clean and perfumed clothes, which are an external means toward spiritual blessings. One should avoid listening to the performance of a singer who indulges in intoxicants; otherwise, constriction and scattering will result instead of expansion and opening up.

Shaykh Ruzbihan Baqli in his *Book of Lights in the Unveiling of Secrets* writes that the singer should be beautiful, since the knowers of God need three things while listening to music in order to give life to their hearts: sweet perfumes, a beautiful face, and a lovely voice. Some Sufis say that a sober singer is better than a beautiful one, since there is danger in the latter.

3. A singer must understand spiritual states and have a subtle sense of taste. With his gaze on the listeners, seeing which verses exert their power over which people, if one person goes into ecstasy from a particular verse, it is essential for him to repeat that verse until that person settles down from ecstasy. How many moments have been constricted and thoughts destroyed because of an ignorant singer! He does not know the spiritual state of someone who is in empathetic ecstasy, the kind of poetry that is appropriate for that spiritual state, or which direction will lead to well-being and which direction to destruction. These days, knowledgeable singers are few. Therefore, while music is being listened to in company, if the singer makes an error, he should be made aware of it.

4. The enunciation and attention of the singer should

be directed toward the people of taste and ecstasy, not toward the rich and powerful because of greedy hopes.

5. It is objectionable for a singer to engage in vocal exercises or to show off his art. This does not mean he should have a bad voice or be a stranger to the art of music. He performs the words along with melody, thinking of the musical modes (*raga, ragini*) and their rhythms.

6. It is necessary to consider the order of presentation of subjects. One begins with praise of God and adoration of the Prophet. At the end, one recites the unity of God. It is difficult to set other moods after reciting the unity of God.

General Guidance

As much as greed is objectionable in the singer, avarice and greed are even more objectionable in the listener. An impoverished singer is excused to a certain extent, for singing is his way of life and his profession. The listener has prayers for the love of God (who is great and mighty), the holy Prophet (may God bless him and grant him peace), and the saints. Another condition for loving God and the Messenger of God is to reject the world and worldly fortune. As Rumi says:

> So you want God and also want the world?
> This is illusory, impossible, insane.

Think about a time when a friend of yours or a special person has sent you a gift, how happy you were, how you were in such a wonderful relationship with the giver, and how he gave something both appropriate for your character and also of significant value and worth. Now that you know that the gift-giver neither gets access nor is denied, there is only one meaning. It is worth considering that the spiritual blessings, the expansiveness of the heart, and the advancement conferred by the eternal court while you are listening to music reach you through an external medium, which is the singer. It is evident that gifts without any real value or worth are not at all appropriate for Him. So imagine what it means if you give the singer nothing. It is totally obvious that you have none of the blessings, nor any of the greatness and reality of God (who is great and mighty) in your heart, that is, you don't have as much as any of your friends or any worldly ruler. Giving nothing to the singer despite your ability to do so is clear proof of the fact that your claim of the love of God and God's Messenger is purely verbal and erroneous, and you are not worthy of listening to music. To you, listening to music is no more than fun and games, and you only listen for enjoyment!

Once an assembly of listening to music was held in the presence of the revered emperor of the masters, who gave the musicians whatever he had. When there was nothing left, he glanced around and saw a tablecloth on a peg; he tied up some bread in it and gave that as well. This is love of God and God's Messenger! It is not that you should be eager to give even silver coins, or that you should claim this love, which is pure vanity. But ask yourself truly if you people have not ruined the singers, who are now forced to fix prices in advance.

When you present a gift to the singer, place it before

your own master. If there is no master in the assembly, present it through another saint of your order, or a member of the assembly, or some other person.

These days, Bakhsha Qawwal, of Barnawa village in the district of Mirath in northern India, is the Hasan Bedi [a famous singer] of the age. All the qualities of Hasan Bedi are found in Bakhsha, who has seized the melody and lit a fire in the hearts of lovers. Even the hardest human heart enters spontaneously into the singing of Bakhsha. If there is a difference between Bakhsha and Hasan Bedi, it is comparable to the difference between the Sufis of that day and the Sufis of this day.

Finally, I ask to be excused for this distracted composition, and I hope that from its pages mystics and singers alike will find benefit.

The sound of hypocritical chant is graceless.
How fine the sound of the flute and the cries of
    drunkards!

6

ETHICAL PRACTICE

THE PRACTICAL ASPECT of Sufism may be viewed under the category of ethics (Arabic *akhlaq*), and indeed Sufism draws upon the ethical teachings of the Greek philosophers to a certain extent. The term *Sufi* was in fact mostly used to signify an ethical ideal that was variously conveyed by many definitions. Sometimes, however, the ideal could be best conveyed by describing what one should *not* do. Spiritual masters observed enough problems over the years, and it was perhaps inevitable that a number of treatises were devoted to the mistakes one should avoid. Ruzbihan Baqli composed one such booklet, in answer to a series of questions, which is translated here. It covers a wide range of problems in five sections, beginning with an extended meditation on the concept of infidelity, the deliberate rejection of God's message that is the most fundamental religious error in the vocabulary of the Qur'an. Ruzbihan applies this concept psychologically to every level of the individual self (the carnal soul, the mind, the heart, and the spirit), so that infidelity becomes a basic metaphor for the assertion of the ego. The carnal soul is an infidel in its rejection of spiritual phenomena such as miracles, the spiritual states of saints, and mystical unveilings. The mind is an infidel because it rejects God's ability to take on visible forms, it rejects God's ability to annihilate the mind, and it rejects the forms that the spirit once worshiped as God. The heart is an infidel whenever it sees duality, whether in its contemplation of God or itself. The spirit is an infidel whenever it has ego consciousness in its enjoyment of spiritual states, in its recollection of God, or in its unwillingness to be effaced.

Next follows the second section, containing a brief discussion on the various kinds of love, and the third section provides a passionate and inspired description of the highest forms of spiritual companionship and friendship. In the fourth section, Ruzbihan goes into considerable detail about the master-disciple relationship, including a brief passage on "the seven jewels," enumerating the characteristics that are essential to a spiritual master. The lengthy fifth section contains a large number of problems that arise in the spiritual path, divided loosely into errors in the essentials of religion and errors in the applications of those principles. Essential errors include flouting the religious law and morality, using specious logic to justify satisfying one's own desires, and mistaking physical sensations for spiritual visions. Errors of application cover a more venal list of sins, such as preferring wealth to poverty, being a hypocritical Sufi, seeking dispensation from the rules, excessive asceticism, love of power, and so forth. The sixth section, a miscellaneous series of questions and sayings, has been omitted from the translation; it appears to be a later addition. Ruzbihan's booklet is a fascinating exposition of the ideals and problems of the spiritual path in Sufism, especially because it appears to be a realistic exposition of problems actually encountered by devotees.

The Errors of Wayfarers
Ruzbihan Baqli

These questions were asked concerning the path of the people of knowledge, and they were answered with the assistance of God, who is powerful and mighty.

Infidelity

The question was asked concerning *the reality of infidelity.*

Know (may God purify you of adverse impurities) that for the devotee, there are four kinds of infidelity that are causally related to psychological and existential disturbances. There is an infidelity of the carnal soul, an infidelity of the mind, an infidelity of the heart, and an infidelity of the spirit.

The infidelity of the carnal soul is of three kinds: an infidelity toward miracles, an infidelity toward spiritual states, and an infidelity toward unveilings.

Now, *the infidelity of the carnal soul toward miracles* is when one is disturbed and doubtful about every divine transformation that appears in the world of action; this is "a character trait of ignorance and blindness." One is blind and deluded about a miracle and doubts it. If you present all the major and minor miracles to such a person, he will not have faith in them. Yes, because of a dominating and wrathful spirit and a reproachful heart (and because of the continuous grace of God on you as a knower of God), for this reason you would say that he is content with deception and delusion, and that he is never able to take part in the secret of his heart. We have no empathy with him, for God has no affection for him. Thus God created him in this fashion, so that he would deflect his gaze from God's existence to the soul's existence; if he had seen God, he would never have become an infidel. This is because all he sees is himself; he does not see God.

This is the infidelity of Pharaoh—without seeing God, he saw himself, and so became an infidel. But whoever looks away from himself toward God becomes an infidel toward His own attributes. The latter (looking to God) is the basis of unity, and the former (looking to oneself) is the basis of infidelity. Sometimes it happens that a man's existence is all carnal soul, and sometimes it happens that his existence is all spirit. Whenever he looks at himself through himself, it is all carnal soul. Whenever he looks at God through God, it is all spirit.

Now, *the infidelity of the carnal soul toward spiritual states* happens when the praise of the spirit descends on someone in the outpouring of love, and the pure divine presence is filled with the joy of holy greatness. The spirit's spirit once again drinks the lordly wine from the spirit's cup with a servant's taste. Without position, it moves into position. From this person's overwhelming passions of love, ecstatic expressions come forth from him. From every atom of that chevalier a tongue bursts into the speech of divine I-ness. But an infidel opposes him, saying, "You are not God." He says this because he does not know God; but whatever the mystic says at that moment, God says. Whatever his tongue expresses, the other unquestionably remains an infidel.

The infidelity of the carnal soul toward unveilings happens when one tears away the veils of the Presence, and the brides of reality appear. On the level of the spirit, divine shapes enter as holy spirits and show themselves to the pure spirit. The wonders of the Kingdom appear from the hidden rarities. The spirit says that this vision is divine unity, but that infidel says that this is just reducing the divine to human terms. This is because imagination is his habit, and he sees the angelic realm with the eye of imagination. Therefore he condemns this, for he does not know that these are the marvels of divine lordship that have appeared in the sources of creaturehood. The carnal soul cannot be called a monotheist, because it is not even a pluralist. The spirit, however, is a monotheist, because it is not born of this earthly way-station. Therefore it has faith in the wonders of God.

The infidelity of the mind is of three types.

The infidelity of the mind toward "clothing with divinity." One form of infidelity concerns the clothing of the divine command with divinity, which is beyond the limit of the mind and understanding, because the mind is a baby in the school of the religious law. The mind rejects and is an infidel to whatever it does not see on the tablet of the religious law. This kind of transcendental experience is found in the tale of Khizr and Moses (Q 18:65–82) (God's prayers be upon them), for that is where the ambiguity lies.

The infidelity of the mind toward its own annihilation by the assaults of the divine wrath. But in another situation of the mind's infidelity, what is intended is the mind that ends up in the world of divine wrath. When the army of divine praise destroys the army of the mind with the assault of divinity at the feast of eternity, it wounds the mind with the scabbard of astonishment. But even though the assault of divinity is said to be eternal, the mind says it is nonexistent. This is because the mind is born of time and place; if the mind were to reach eternity, the infinite would become finite, because it would become the vessel of time. The permanence of God's infinite existence is unique in existence. There is no path to this desert for any creature. The four companions who are laborers in the market of God (a symbol for the carnal soul, mind, heart, and spirit) have no power on this playing field, because God is the one who is his own existence. No one knows God's existence except by his existence. Mind is a stranger to him, because in reality it is mad.

The infidelity of the mind toward the forms that the spirit worshiped. But in another situation, in which the mind is overwhelmed by the divine unity, that is the station of omnipotence, in which the One is transcendent. The spirit has no power there, because the spirit is in a defined station. When, beyond the veils of the angelic realm, it sees the kindness of the encounter with divine lordshi, in the world of destinies, and it sees the handwritten letter of the Beloved, the spirit thinks that it has grasped the ungraspable, and, like Abraham seeing the sunrise, it says, "This is my Lord" (Q 6:76). This is the means to witnessing, even though it is only the gateway to unveiling, because in the end the spirit says like Abraham, "I am going to my Lord, who will guide me" (Q 37:99).

But the mind was only at the beginning of divine unity in the separate abode of destinies. From haste, its alertness became confusion. With every dawning that arose deceptively from the orients of omnipotence, the mind said, "This is my Lord" (Q 6:76). Abraham's request was "Let me see" (Q 2:260), since it was the beginning of vision. Therefore when the veil fell from the Truth in God's reply, "Do you not believe?" (Q 2:260), Abraham (peace be upon him) said, "Yes, but I ask to pacify my heart" (Q 2:260).

Because the mind is weak in relation to the divine unity, when it realized that vision has to be clothed in forms of divinity, it knew that this was not pure unity. Like Abraham seeing the sunset, it said, "I renounce the things that you associate with God! I have turned my face to the Creator of the Heavens and the earth as a true worshiper" (Q 6:78–79).

The infidelity of the heart occurs at three times: at the time of meditation, at the time of encounter with God, and at the time of self-examination.

The infidelity of the heart in meditation. When one meditates and his gaze falls upon the Truth, by that inclination he is an infidel (since sight is still in the realm of duality).

The infidelity of the heart in encountering God. When one enters an encounter with God, if one asks God for anything but God, or repeats anything about oneself to God, he is an infidel.

The infidelity of the heart in self-examination. At the time of self-examination, when purifying the inner secrets, one is veiled from illuminations, because one is occupied with something other than God. One reckons them up as the reality of one's own actions. Whoever so limits them is an infidel. If one does not see God as the actor in each act, he is an infidel.

The infidelity of the spirit is the infidelity that is the essence of divine unity. Yes, it is a means to him, because it is at the beginning of the world of destiny, and it appears in three states.

The infidelity of the spirit in enjoyment. If the spirit takes enjoyment in love, it is an infidel, because it is held back from God by enjoyment.

The infidelity of the spirit in recollection. Another state: when one becomes intimate with the recollection of God's names, one should know that the act of recollection is not the same as the one who is recollected. If one is veiled from the recollected one by recollection, that is the essence of infidelity.

The infidelity of the spirit in fleeing effacement. Another state is when the authority of the divine beauty reaches him: it reduces him to nothing, because he cannot bear the glories of the divine essence. If one does not seek efface-ment but flees into sobriety, he is an infidel.

This is the infidelity of the knowers of God. If an atom of it were to be scented by the souls of all the infidels, they all would become believers in the one God, because infidelity is a covering for Him. If you do not reach Him, you are an infidel to Him. If you reach Him, you are an infidel to yourself. You do not reach Him until you become an infidel to yourself; reach Him, and become a believer in His unity. As long as you remain yourself, you are still in forms animated by spirits. As long as you remain yourself, infidelity and faith are two separate things. But when God's existence manifests itself, it takes away both infidelity and Islam.

This is because separation is a hundred thousand unions. As long as you don't consume the bitterness of infidelity, you won't taste the sweetness of the honey of divine unity. If you don't get the slap of wrath, He won't give you the pleasure of grace. Infidelity is by His wish, and beneath His blanket there are a hundred thousand maddened wise men. By the soul of all noble youths! Every hour I become an infidel a million times, and then once again I become a Muslim. What I knew, I didn't know, and what I saw, I didn't see. What do you say? A hidden one is present, and a present one is hidden. If I am with myself, I am an infidel, and hidden. If I am with Him, I am a believer in God's unity, and present. When I am with Him, I am without him. All is He, and all is without Him. If He shows Himself to you, you will see. If He speaks to you, you will know. And God knows best.

Passionate Love and Love

. . . He was also asked about passionate love (*'ishq*) and love (*mahabba*) and its reality.

He said, Know (may God grant you success on the lovers' path) that the beginning of passionate love is love, and then comes longing, the limit of which is passionate love, or drowning in love. All three of these follow upon unveiling and witnessing, because when uninterrupted graces reach the heart by means of illuminations from God's hidden world, the heart is filled with the love of God. When the emanation of His beauty is continuous, His longing appears. When there is intoxication in the beauty and majesty of the holy spirit, His love appears. The cause of the intoxication of the spirit is the affliction of the spirit by the beauty of God.

The source of love is the purity of the attributes. When one sees God with the ornament of eternal beauty, he is a lover of God. Not every one who is happy is a lover, and not every one who is intimate is a lover. Love has no limit, because the beauty of the Beloved has no limit. Love arises from this; what follows on that is the dawning of divine unity.

And love in divine unity is the station of infidelity, because in love there is duality. If the lover is single in the divine unity, whom can he love? When the distracted soul finds rest from the events of the hidden, it will see beyond, to the marvels of the hidden of the hidden, with the eye's vision. When its existence becomes all eye, when nothing but the eye remains in existence, it will ride the steed of compassion to eternal exile, because it can take the baggage of separation to the meeting place of union. Then it is utterly stripped by love, for the reality of love is found in the secret of eternal divine presence (where there is no lover).

That annihilation is the cradle of the infant spirit; the hand of divine greatness is made transcendent by divine unity.

If beauty agitates love, rarity agitates reality, and the purity of the divine attributes is there (when the lover vanishes). When that lover's desire is effaced (along with the lover), he reaches God's attributes, for that is love. Love is one of God's attributes, and being a lover is His profession; He Himself is the lover, and He is of the same color as love.

Companionship

He was also asked about companionship.

He said, Know (may God give you success in the companionship of the sincere and the upright) that companionship is the firm fortress of divine knowledge, and it is also the assembly that gathers in the holy enclosures of divine unity. As God said (who is transcendent and lofty), "There is no secret conversation of three without God as the fourth" (Q 58:7). It is the bankruptcy market of the carnal soul, and the cattle auction of the holy spirit. It is the pure crucible of the goldsmith of the soul; when one leaves the mines of natural Islam, one gets stamped in that mint. Companionship is the way-station of the purification of secrets, and it is also the place where the suns of illumination rise. That is where they remove natural misfortunes from the clay of the children of Adam.

They are strange princes who go into the exile of annihilation with each other. They raise up everything other than sheer servanthood in pure lordship, with the hand of sincerity, to the paths of divine knowledge. They are the dwellers of the realm of "those who give ear" (Q 50:37), and they are the knights of the hidden world. Those who are prophets for each other from God—if you see them, in form they are different, but they are single in soul. You see them all, and you see no other, for you will find no otherness with them.

They are the spies of hearts, and the mirrors of the hidden. They are born of the mother of compassion, and therefore they are tender with each other. They are helpers of God, since they assist each other. They take turns in all things from their equality, and they pray for each other in their supplications. From uprightness they are straight with their friends and crooked with themselves. Their secrets are open to each other, since they are not strangers to each other. They are the sources of the caravan of scented breezes, and they are the ones who inhale the wind of holy fragrance. In their market they sell rare wonders of the angelic realm, and no one buys but those who sell. They are each other's prayer direction when they are in isolation. Their only weapon is contention, and in contention they find harmony. As the Master Muhammad said (God bless him and grant him peace), "Difference among scholars is a mercy."

Their attribute is preferring others, and sincerity is their garment. They are the soul of each other, and when they are apart they are lifeless. They are agreeable in their association, speaking without the carnal soul and listening with the heart. They appoint the realities of their inner secrets to reckon up the number of each other's breaths. They are attentive to meeting with each other. At the time of conviviality they are all sober. Friendship is their profession, truth-

fulness is their pasture, and sincerity is their meadow. In
their favorite company they do not wound each other, for
they know that injuring each other is injuring themselves.
They are in union at the time of separation, and separation
is banished among them.

From truthfulness and sincerity, they do not merely tol-
erate each other, nor do they flee each other when they
hold conversation. All are servants of each other, and all
are teachers of each other. All are disciples of each other,
because they are in essence one. When companionship appears, it brings stability; even when it is disturbed, in all
conditions it is to be chosen. It is the trace of God, for it is
the representative of God to his creation.

Whoever becomes more perfect through companionship
becomes on his own account the representative of his time.
"Abraham was a nation" (Q 16:120). One becomes the guide
and the guided one when one has the inheritance of the
prophets. If there were no companionship, man would not
be rooted in the commands of lordship, would not be at
rest in the flow of fate and destiny, and would not be literate and learned in the assemblies of intimacy. Their meal
companion is someone who eats the bread of wild herbs,
and who consumes hunger with them. One who sleeps with
them shares their breath both day and night in meditation's
breathing. They are the people of God's house, among
whom there is no stranger. This is because they are the
brides of the hidden way-station, and they have the precious jewels of wisdom. No one but themselves should hear
their words, for if others hear, they will be tempted. The
condition of companionship is the condition of divine

knowledge. Those who go within themselves become more knowing, and more truthful, in companionship.

The Master and the Disciple

He was also asked about the master and the disciple.

He said, Know (may God grant you success) that the disciple is the archer's arrow that speeds from the bow of guidance, which does not hit the target of pleasure at any station. He is the one caught in the noose of love, who is pinned by the spikes of longing. He is the one astonished in the deserts of sorrow, who is the camel that has lost the way. He suffers the loss of ecstasy, and in ecstasy he is lost. He has no direction, because he is disoriented. Externally he is mature, but in reality he is raw. His nature is receptive in love, and his soul is at rest.

Servanthood is his ornament, and the affirmation of lordship is his shadow. He is overwhelmed, isolated, meditative, present, recollecting, repentant, abstemious, ascetic, devout, pure, truthful, sincere, penitent, compassionate. He is a helper of friends and a companion to those who suffer. He is noble in the pain of faith, peerless in trusting God, a ruler in the heart's kingdom. He strives without ceasing, he is a veil without hope, he is happy without vision. He is unified, strange, and single. He is consumed.

His morals are noble, and his tongue is subtle. He is submissive, benign, and merciful. He does not flee from affliction, and when he tastes real meanings, he does not mix them with desires. When love's sorrow is appropriate, he is a spark from the fire of the masters. He is the disciple (*murid*) and potentially the master (*murad*); were it not for the latter, he would not appear. The disciple is a disciple in servanthood and a master in lordship. There is no ease in discipleship, nor any impurity in the disciple.

The master reaches the stage of mastery when he becomes the knower and practitioner of seven of the jewels of the path. First is to be in servanthood while undergoing dangers, and to succeed in keeping deliverance in view. A man does not become perfect in the path of mystical knowledge until he understands the temptations of the devil, and his tricks, and knows the carnal soul's muttering and its mockeries. As Muhammad, the Master of the worlds, and the lord of "two bow lengths" (Q 53:9), said (God's blessings and peace be upon him), "Whoever knows his self has known his Lord."

The master does not become a knower of God if he has not recognized problems, for problems befall the person who is free of problems. Although problems are more numerous than the stars in Heaven, the sands of the desert, drops of rain, or the hairs of living things, still a few words will be said as far as possible, which may be useful to seekers, God willing.

Of all the errors of this community, the most obvious is when disciples are opinionated and pleased with themselves and they seek no example from any master. They say, "We will be our own master." They have one, but it is the devil. As it is said, "One who has no master has Satan for a leader."

Another of their errors is that they do not know the science of the religious law, and they consider its study to be shameful. They claim that the science of the religious law is harmful to the path. From foolishness they do not know that they do not know.

Another of their errors is that they do not observe good manners under all circumstances, and all of their actions become crimes. They think that they have reached the goal, but it is Hellfire.

Another of their errors is that they perform the supplementary prayers and devotions, but they become lazy and neglect the obligatory ones, and they criticize the pious worshiper, saying that the worshiper is not perfect. They are overthrown by the carnal soul. They have no idea that the *seven jewels* are necessary; when these are attained, a man is a knower of God, and he knows how to attain the following things:

1. Traveling the road to lordship by servanthood and its specific properties.
2. Being refined and purified by the path, and knowing errors and how to avoid them.
3. Attaining all the sciences of the religious law, and implementing its realities with true knowledge and practice.
4. Grasping mystical knowledge and having insight into it.
5. Knowing the science of spiritual states and their rules.
6. Understanding the science of unveilings and their realities.
7. Attaining the utmost witnessing and diving into the oceans of divine unity, and then becoming firmly fixed in the rules and limits of mystical knowledge.

Everyone in whom these seven realities appear is suitable for and capable of mastery. For mastery is an inheritance from God, by which he reveals himself to disciples. That person is God's representative, and from his beautiful face, life itself increases. He is schooled in the manners of God, he knows by the instruction of God, and he acts by the command of God. He is intimate in passionate love, unique in the divine unity, and rooted in mystical knowledge.

He is the nest of the birds of aspiration, the Heaven of knowledge for the constellations and the planets, the desert spark of flashing lights, the example for seekers of witnessing, and the key to the treasury of unveiling. He is the touchstone for all disciples; they take whomever he takes, and they reject whomever he rejects.

Problems of the Path

He was also asked about the problems of the path and its errors.

He answered, saying, Know (may God preserve you from the trials of the Sufis who are called to prayer) that the problems and errors of the path are more numerous than can be told. Their number is according to the number of the souls of wayfarers, for in every soul there is an error, just as in every soul there is a guidance and direction. No one comprehends their ambiguity except a divine master who has knowledge of the hidden realm.

One of their errors is that they take delight in pleasures,

and say that this is joy. But it is delirium, for joy is good manners.

Another problem is that they do not care about forbidden and doubtful things, saying that lawful and forbidden apply only to those who have not reached the goal. Although in the divine oneness all is one, this saying of theirs is pure ignorance and an abdication of free will and accountability. The creature is accountable and is responsible to God for all actions.

The greatest of their errors is that they sit with women and youths and have contact with one another, and think themselves unharmed. To be sure, love brings desire to any place where it descends in a state of witnessing. When nothing of mortality remains in all the being of the wayfarer, it is safe for him to sit in the assemblies of the lovers of God. And there is a group that from infidelity declares that wine is lawful, saying, "It is our vehicle." It is a disgraceful state when one has a need for "bitter water" (wine), for the intoxication of real men is from witnessing the beauty of God, which produces agitation in the soul of lovers.

One of their errors is that they neglect every religious duty that God (glory be to Him who is transcendent) has required of His creatures, such as ritual prayer, fasting, alms, charity, and the like. They represent themselves, saying, "We are distinguished by freedom, and servanthood does not concern us."

Another of their errors is that while they have not yet been in servanthood, they speak of lordship. Lordship is the state of intoxication, and servanthood is the state of sobriety. As long as the knowers of God are in this world, both lordship and servanthood are indispensable for them. The sign of the state of lordship is whenever intoxication enters: "Do not approach prayer when you are intoxicated" (Q 4:43). The sign of the state of servanthood is whenever sobriety enters: "The messiah will not scorn to be the slave of God, nor will the near angels" (Q 4:172).

Another of their errors is that they hold that ablutions for prayer, ritual purity, and cleansings for impurity are of no account; they say, "We have the ablution of pre-eternity." They have something, but it is the impurity of pre-eternity, from which all the seas of the world will not purify them. As Muhammad, the master of the world and the chosen one of the sons of Adam (blessings and peace be upon him), said, "If the people of Sodom used the waters of oceans for ablution, they would still arrive impure on Resurrection Day." This is because the holiness of ritual purity is an attribute of God, and the pure ones love the holy. "God loves the repentant, and He loves those who purify themselves" (Q 2:222).

Another of their errors is that they backbite, and they repeat slander outside the balance of religious law. They are attached to it, and they mix it with mockeries and outrages, setting themselves apart with these words. They are satans to one another, and they greedily seize the harm of Satan, being his followers, for God (the great and mighty) said there are "Satans both of men and jinn" (Q 6:112).

The greatest of their sins is that if you place the correct path before them, they do not accept it. From their nature and their desire, they are incapable of it, and they say, "We have witnessed infidelity from our friends, parents, and leaders." They are in agreement with those infidels who said, "We found our fathers in a religion, and we are following in their footsteps" (Q 43:23).

One of their errors is that they say, "Whatever was in pre-eternity we cannot change, and no alteration or change can take place in that at our request." And by these words they take the path of delightful pleasure, and their words are fine but their deeds are foul. The proof against them is that they flee in time of pain and affliction. If their speech were on a par with their intention, they would have accepted everything as the command of pre-eternity. Why do they like some things and not others? "We believe in some things and we reject others" (Q 4:150) is their profession. Their intention by these words is to abrogate ritual actions, and to choose pleasure, the desires of the world, and the nullification of religion: these are the origins of the sect of atheism. Whoever says these things has an opinion close to the sect of atheism. Let us flee to God for protection from their sect!

One of their errors is that they are preoccupied with libertinism. They say, "The doer of all these deeds is God; we have no power over these things." Thus they make lawful the permitting of unlawful things. Very quickly they turn toward infidelity.

So it is. The actor and creator of the actions of all existing things is God. He is the creator of all beautiful and despicable things. But what He approved in pre-eternity by granting His eternal satisfaction was beneficent deeds. And what He cast into the Hell of error with His pre-eternal wrath was evil deeds. It is the saying of the transcendent One (who is great and mighty), "Those whom God guides are well guided, and those whom God leads astray are the losers" (Q 7:178).

One of their errors is that they say, "All is He." By saying "all," they take various temporal parts for the essence. By ciphers they say to one another, "We are He." So for these infidels there are a hundred thousand gods, but the Truth (glory be to Him) transcends the joining and separation of temporal things. He is a unity to which there is no path save by Him. He has no dimension, and does not suffer change. By such words they become infidels. They know neither God nor themselves, for if someone were God, how would he ever cease to exist?

There is a group who are in error regarding the spirit, or rather, their error is not regarding the spirit but the body. They say that the spirit is one of the divine essences. They hold the creed of the Christians, which God rejects. Another group says that the elite spirit is His existence, and the general spirit is His creation. This fancy is impossible, for the eternal existence would thus come under limitation and fit into a human vessel. This belief is close to reincarnation, which God opposes.

Another error is that of the weak souls who have imaginations in this world and who see likenesses that they imagine to be unveiling, and which they liken to the essence and attributes of God. They are fanciers and worshipers of the imagination (let us flee to God for protection from their unfortunate thought).

One of their errors is that they consider the saints to be

superior to the prophets, or on the same level; thus they became infidels. This is a corrupt idea. What they say on this subject is that the spiritual state of the prophet is mediated, while the spiritual state of the saint is unmediated. From misunderstanding, this view goes to the limit of ignorance, for the prophets eternally have inspiration, divine discourse, and intimate conversation with God. They are also distinguished by contact with the spirit and message of Gabriel (peace be upon him) and the sending of Scriptures. The spiritual state of prophets is even beyond the spirits in their pure holiness. The state of the saint is overwhelmingly between spirits and forms, and that person knows what he has.

Another of their errors is that a group of them claim to have spiritual visions with the physical eye. That is not possible in the world, and there is a Prophetic tradition about this. There are some who do not distinguish ocular unveiling from spiritual unveiling, and they imagine that whatever they see has itself been seen with the physical eye, but because of their extreme immaturity they cannot recognize what has occurred. A report has come from the Prophet (God bless him and grant him peace) that Iblis (Satan) sits on a throne between Heaven and earth, and he shows himself to a group of ordinary people in order to delude them, and he has an effect on all of them. If they provide any sign of that experience, it is not from God, for God is without sign.

Another of their errors is that a party of them see a certain created light, and they think that light is God, and they connect it with His essence. This is mistaken, for although

He has the quality of light, His light is direction, knowledge, unity, and guidance. But God is beyond the light and darkness of which they speak. Now, God has lights that are beyond all that, yet they are outside of imagination. If God manifested himself to creation with likenesses of His own glory, to the degree that God Himself knows it (which does not enter the limits of how or when), all existing beings would be consumed. He is astonishing in every state, and the light of His majesty is eternal. The rational spirit, which is the spirit of majesty and divine holiness, has the quality of this light of divine manifestation. Whoever sees, sees by that, knows by that, speaks by that, hears by that, and grasps by that. In the holy Qur'an, it is by this likeness to God (who is mighty and powerful) that He thus spoke: "God is the light of the Heavens and the earth" (Q 24:35).

Another of their errors is that they become implicated in misleading others, and when time passes by, they cannot depart from that, from the power of hypocrisy and the awareness of the gaze of others. When one has made a claim to spiritual authority, and has traveled this road for a time, people have seen him in that fashion and have praised him. But since he is a prisoner of ego and hypocrisy, he finds that path of infidelity pleasing to him. He is ashamed to follow the right path, lest he be despised in the eyes of the people. For when one enters the law of the Prophet (God bless him and grant him peace), one must become a laborer. But this evildoer finds himself greatly honored by the people. And the commands of the religious law are weighty, and they humiliate the carnal soul. But the wealthy, from their extreme love of possessions, cast off the inconvenience of duty, for the burden of the law is a heavy burden for them. "It is hard except for the humble" (Q 2:45).

Everything that has been said so far regarding the errors of this community consists of certain errors regarding the essentials of religion, by which religion is devastated. But the errors that fall in the applications of religion we shall also explain by way of example, so that the right way is distinguished from losing the way on this path in a given time (if it is the will of God, Most High and One).

Now among the errors that fall into the applications, one is that they consider the wealthy to be superior to the poor, and they do not know that the Lord of the universe has chosen the poverty and asceticism of the wayfarers for himself, saying, "God is better and more lasting" (Q 20:73). He also praised the sincere, saying, "Alms for the poor who restrain themselves for God's cause" (Q 2:273). The best of Adam's children, the chosen one of the world, Muhammad the favored one (may God bless him and grant him peace), chose poverty for himself and his people, passing by the world and its trash, saying, "Poverty is my pride."

And another of their errors is that a group of them place upon themselves the sign of the Sufis, though they are ignorant of their spiritual state, and they satisfy themselves with name and appearance. In this form some of them parade themselves with flattery and advertisement, and they sell something they do not own. "God does not guide the deceit of the treacherous" (Q 12:52).

There is a group that choose acquisition of material goods as their spiritual state, and they condemn the state of trust in God for all things. They do not know that trust in God was the spiritual state of the Prophet (may God bless him and grant him peace), while acquisition was only his practice. Trust in God is for the strong, and acquisition is for the weak. But anyone who attains and comprehends his own state avoids denigrating and slandering others.

There is a group that say the next world may be better reached by this world than by poverty. Thus they seek a dispensation, so that they may fall into pleasure and desires. It should be known that by asceticism and isolation one finds a better reward than by attachments and impediments.

Another of their errors is that, when they are unable to bear the weight of the path of blame and dervishhood in the wide world, they therefore look for dispensation and interpretation. Yes, when they are not authentic, from extreme deception they make interpretations their shield.

Another of their errors is that, when they hear mention of the great masters and they understand their nobility next to God (who is great and mighty), therefore they attempt to imitate their ascetic exercises, and they continue to do them for a long time. They find no sweetness in that, and they find no peace in God Most High, nor do they find respect from the people. The mood of asceticism sits upon them, and all the people flee from them, because they have entered with deception and departed with laziness. They do not know that "God Most High contends with them on that."

Another of their errors is that a group of them intend to visit various cities, so that they may tell of what may be seen, thus gaining honor and respect. The true lovers of the past were not such as this. May God be pleased with those true lovers, and may he pour for their spirits the wine of his favor.

Another of their errors is that they give away money and display their generosity, trying to serve people so that by this means they may gain the office of chief shaykh. The bygone masters (may God have mercy on them) gave up honor by way of wealth, and they bestowed themselves upon their friends. They departed from the path of exchange, for exchange is forbidden in the path of lovers.

Another of their errors is that a party of them say, "We are detached from the world. We can do whatever we encounter." They do not distinguish between truth and falsehood, lawful and unlawful. This saying is the key to their vanity, for by it they open the door to libertinism.

Another of their errors is that a group of beggars hears about the miracles of the Sufis, and they think that this comes about through ascetic striving. They do not know that together with ascetic striving, one needs the capacity for miracles and the assistance of God (who is great and mighty). When they do some of that, and nothing happens, they reject the miracles of the saints. This is a sign of stupidity, not a sign of ascetic striving. Ascetic striving in God brings about miracles, because ascetic striving in the manner of religious law is the path of guidance.

Another of their errors is that a certain group from ignorance weaken themselves through excessive asceticism, to the extent that they abstain from required religious duties.

They do not know that the masters perform asceticism gradually, not in haste.

Another error is that of the recluses living in mountains or caves without the spiritual state or station of the masters. Their fancy is that they have fled from the people and have applied themselves to demanding ascetic practices by which they have become safe from the evil of the carnal soul. They do not realize that one cannot ever become safe from the evil of the carnal soul. The Sufis cannot sit in seclusion without a spiritual state; otherwise, the disease of melancholy would become greater than spiritual states or unveiling.

Another of their errors is that a group have made themselves into eunuchs. They think by doing that they escape the affliction of desires. They do not know that desires are not in the instrument, rather desires are in the constitution; as long as the latter exists, the former exists.

Another of their errors is that some people have dispensed with provisions and caravans in the desert, and they have perished. They did not know that when the masters went to the desert, their souls were pledged to the love of God, and their hearts were full of trust in God and certainty. To them, being hungry or full, ruined or thriving, was the same.

Another of their errors is that a group become preoccupied with ceremony and clothing, and they dress in dyed clothes and colored garments, sitting in hospices and teaching the allusions of the Sufis. They think that they also are Sufis. Negligence overcomes them, and they fail to live up to the demands and examples of Sufism. On the Day of

Judgment, sorrow, repentance, Hellfire, and reproach will be their burden.

Another error is that a group fill treasuries with goods of the world, with dirhams and dinars, employing them for profits and partnerships, finding solace in that kind of good. Despite all that, they perform ritual prayer and keep all fasts, demonstrating their piety and tears. They say that one needs goods so that worship remains on a sound basis, and so that the heart is not distracted but remains at ease. They imagine that this is the spiritual condition of the elite. What a vain fancy this is! How could the reality of servant-hood exist without self-denial? Until you dispense with attachments and impediments, your servanthood will not be correct.

Another of their errors is that a party of maniacs choose dancing, verses, music, clapping, and rending garments as their path. They imagine that when this is achieved, they have attained the state of the saints. By these falsehoods one cannot discover spiritual stations.

Another error is that a group of them say, "The reality of purity is to restrain oneself from ever seeing the world of humanity; otherwise one cannot attain purity." By this they mean that from the external perspective, purity means they become cut off from humanity, but that is sheer fancy. But one who is distinguished by purity would experience none of the dust of otherness in his pure vision even if all creation and humanity came into his vision at once.

Another error is that a number of them do not understand the truth of theology. They think that annihilation means the annihilation of one's humanity, and they fall into various types of headache and melancholy. Some advocate abstaining from food and drink, in order to make themselves thin, and they imagine that annihilation is the annihilation of the pleasure of the soul by God in utter unity. But annihilation consists of annihilation from annihilation.

These errors of theirs in the applications they have performed have brought them to a dangerous situation for religious aspirants. Errors also befall them on the journey toward spiritual realities; when these befall them, they are veiled from the secrets of spiritual stations and the realities of spiritual states. We shall clarify some of these issues, if God alone wishes.

Now, the errors that befall wayfarers on the journey to spiritual abodes include weeping without burning, complaint without longing, presence without nearness, expansion without respect, empathetic ecstasy without ecstasy, sobriety without intoxication, sadness without happiness, fear without hope, hope without fear, listening to music without pain, discipleship without desire, contraction without expansion, desolation without intimacy, laughing without weeping, teasing without sweetness, meditation without unveiling, imagination without uncovering, allusion without mystical knowledge, clothing with divinity without love, seeking forgiveness without penitence, repentance without contrition, worry without good news, crying without tears, trembling without ecstasy, dreaming without playfulness, dawning without enchantment, obliteration without burial, dancing without agitation, love without bewilderment, seizing without adornment, authority without testing, servanthood without lordship, warning without jealousy, longing without demanding death, going to God's desert without provision, seeking love without fragrance, listening to music without melody, gazing at the bodies of youths without witnessing mercy, spiritual station without state, spiritual state without union, nonexistence without eternity, wandering without suffering, and accepting approved things in the guise of rejected things. This is because on the journey toward spiritual stations and the performance of practices, just as there are useful accepted things, so there are useful rejected things. This allusion is known only by those worthy of the allusion. Peace be upon those who follow guidance.

7

MASTERY AND
DISCIPLESHIP

O NE OF THE CORNERSTONES of the Sufi tradition was
the master-disciple relationship, which over time was
a means of insuring that the spiritual blessings given to the
Prophet Muhammad would continue from generation to
generation. This relationship is probably the most important topic of Sufi handbooks. A good summary of it is contained in the appendix to one of the most famous of all
treatises on Sufism, "The Testament to Disciples" at the
end of the *Epistle* of Abu al-Qasim al-Qushayri (d. 1074).
Al-Qushayri, a native of Iran who wrote in Arabic, in this
treatise gave brief biographical sketches of the early Sufi
masters, along with detailed descriptions of the spiritual
states and stages of the Sufi path.

The passage translated here takes the form of an ethical
testament, a literary genre in which one attempted to distill
the essence of a lifetime's wisdom. Like other early Sufi
authors, he insisted upon linking the practice of Sufism
with the legal and ethical observances of Islam. Nevertheless, he insists that the Sufi master is on a level far higher
than any of the legal scholars, and he maintains that spiri-

tual advancement is generally impossible without a master. In order to take advantage of a relationship with a master, disciples must begin by repenting all sins, and by becoming detached from wealth, popularity, and power. Masters in turn must instruct their disciples according to the differences in their individual temperaments, taking account of qualities such as intelligence and perseverance.

Repeatedly al-Qushayri states that theoretical learning and study of books are not very useful for spiritual advancement. Instead, he recommends practices that tend to reduce the size of the ego. Among these practices, one of the most important is to serve the needs of those who are already traveling the path. In the translation of this passage, I have retained the common Arabic term for a practicing Sufi: *faqir* (literally "poor man"; the Persian equivalent is *darvish*, which is anglicized as *dervish*; both terms basically describe a beggar or religious mendicant who has renounced the world). The beginner needed to spend a time of apprenticeship literally acting as a servant to the Sufi community, as a way of learning humility. The practical and ethical emphasis of all this advice is remarkable. Al-Qushayri is adamant that purity of character is of far greater importance then mere repetition of acts of devotion. He also warns disciples to avoid getting a false sense of their own importance due to unusual spiritual experiences, which in many cases are tests of the aspirant's ability to avoid distractions from the goal, and he cautions them that spiritual masters are not necessarily infallible. All this is a salutary remedy against spiritual vanity.

The Testament to Disciples
ABU AL-QASIM AL-QUSHAYRI

The master and teacher al-Qushayri said: When we set forth a portion of the path of the Sufis, and we added to that several chapters on spiritual stations, we wanted to conclude this treatise with points of advice for disciples. We hope that God Most High will assist them to apply these successfully, that He will not prevent us from setting them forth, and that He (glory be to Him) will not make them a test for us.

The first step on this path for a disciple should be in sincerity, so that his foundation will be set on a correct principle. For the masters have said, "Union with God is prevented only by neglect of principles."

Likewise I heard the master Abu 'Ali al-Daqqaq saying, "It is necessary at the beginning to have correct faith between him and God Most High, so he is purified from fancies and doubts, is emptied of error and innovation, and abandons logical demonstrations and proofs."

It is detestable for a disciple to be connected with a legal school not associated with this spiritual path. The connection of the Sufis is not with one of the competing schools, but with the Sufi path, except when they are ignorant about the teachings of this path. For the Sufis' proofs in answer to questions are clearer than the proofs of anyone else, and the basis of their teachings is more powerful than the basis of any other school.

Ordinary people are either custodians of tradition and

text, or else experts at thought and reflection. The masters of Sufism go beyond all of these. What is hidden to ordinary people is evident to them, and what is an object of study to ordinary folk is for them discovered directly from God (glory be to Him). They are the people of union, but ordinary folk are the people of reasoning.

During the entire Islamic era, there has always been a master of Sufism who possessed the science of unity. At all times, under the leadership of the Sufis, the leading scholars of the age have submitted to that master, humbling themselves to him and asking his blessing.

The principles of the Sufi path are the most correct principles, their masters are the greatest of men, and the Sufi scholars are the most learned of men. Therefore, if the disciple who has faith in the Sufis is a wayfarer progressing toward their goals, he shares with the Sufis in the unveilings of the hidden that distinguish them. He should not be a hanger-on of someone who has left Sufism. If he aspires to follow the path, and has no particular spiritual state, but desires to ascend to the homelands of tradition until he reaches realization, let him follow the tradition of his forebears and pursue the path of Sufism. They are more important to him than anyone else.

When the disciple is establishing the covenant between himself and God, it is necessary for him to acquire knowledge of the religious law, either by experience, or by asking the masters what is required of him. If the decrees of the jurists conflict, he takes the most comprehensive approach, with the purpose of avoiding conflict. But dispensations in religious law are for the feeble, the needy, and the preoccupied.

Sufism has no practice but reliance on the truth of God (glory be to Him). Therefore it is said that when the seeker declines from the stage of reality to the dispensation of religious law, his covenant with God is abolished, and the covenant establishing his relation with God Most High is destroyed.

Thus it is necessary for the disciple to study with a master, and if he does not have a master, he will never succeed. Abu Yazid said, "One who has no master has Satan for a leader."

I heard the master Abu 'Ali say, "The tree that grows by itself without a gardener puts forth leaves, but it does not bear fruit. Similar is the disciple who has no master from whom he can learn his path, one breath at a time. He remains a worshiper of his own desire and does not attain success."

Then, after all this, if one still desires to be a wayfarer, it is necessary for him to turn back to God (glory be to Him) and to turn away from every sin. He must give up all sins, both open and hidden, great and small. He strives to satisfy his opponents first, for one who does not satisfy his opponents will not receive anything from this path.

If one wants to abandon attachments, the first step is to abandon wealth, for wealth makes one incline away from God. Every disciple who enters this mystical enterprise with a worldly attachment finds that this attachment pulls him in the opposite direction. But if he abandons wealth, then abandoning power is also necessary, for even a moment of love of power is a great obstacle.

It is not a matter of indifference if the disciple is accepted by the public, though their rejection is of no consequence. Rather, the thing most harmful to him is if people give him attention with total confidence, and they seek his blessings for the poor because of this reputation. Since he has not been correct as a disciple, how can it be correct to seek his blessing?

Abandoning power is necessary for the wayfarers, since power is a violent poison for them. When one abandons wealth and power, then it is necessary to return to the correct covenant with God Most High. And one should not oppose his master in anything that he is told, because the disciple's opposition at the beginning of his career is gravely harmful, for his beginning state is an indication of his whole life.

And when a master leads someone, it is necessary to instruct him in the formula of recollection that the master sees as appropriate for him. The master orders him to recite that name of God with the tongue, then he tells him to put his heart into harmony with his tongue. He says to him, "Persist in continuous recitation of this as though you are eternally with your Lord in your heart, so that no other name but this will be on your tongue or will be possible for you to say." Then he orders him to be always in a state of external purity, to sleep only when necessary, and gradually to reduce his food little by little until he can withstand that. He does not order him to abandon his habits all at once, for a tradition of the Prophet states, "The reckless rider who rides an animal to death covers no ground and retains no mount." Then he tells him to choose seclusion and isolation, and in this state he begins his efforts to deny the worldly thoughts and concerns that occupy the heart.

Know that, in this state, the disciple who is free from misgivings in his belief at the times of seclusion in the beginning of his discipleship undoubtedly has an intelligent heart. Indeed, there are few disciples who fail to encounter such misgivings at the beginning of their discipleship. This is one of the tests that disciples face. If the master sees intelligence in the disciple, he should assign him to study intellectual proofs from theology, for religious knowledge undoubtedly purifies the knowledgeable person from being overpowered by misgivings.

If the master intuitively perceives that the disciple has strength and perseverance on the path, he orders him to continue patiently with recitation of God's name until the lights of divine acceptance shine in his heart, and the suns of union dawn in his conscience: that will take place soon. But this only occurs with a few disciples. Generally the remedy for their problems is through rejecting theoretical approaches. Study of scriptural passages for the acquisition of knowledge of juristic principles depends on the level of need appropriate to the disciple.

If God desires good for a disciple, He confirms it at the beginning of discipleship. If God desires a bad end for a disciple, He returns him to the profession or condition that he had departed from. If God desires tribulation for a disciple, He drives him away to abodes of exile.

It is very harmful to the disciple of medium ability if he

joins the *faqir*s and companions while still a beginner. If anyone is tested in that fashion, however, he should take the path of respect for the masters, serving the companions, abandoning opposition to them, relying on what pleases *faqir*s, and striving not to trouble the master's heart. Whenever he is in the company of *faqir*s he should only oppose himself and never oppose others. He should see that every one of them has an obligatory right over him, and that none has an obligation to him. The disciple should not contradict anyone, and even if he knows that he is right, he is silent. He acts in agreement with everyone.

If the disciple is prone to laughter, stubbornness, or contentiousness, it will do him no good. If the disciple is with a group of *faqir*s, whether on a journey or at home, it is not proper for him to contradict them openly, neither when eating nor when asking, neither at rest nor in motion. Rather, he may contradict them in his conscience and his heart, for he entrusts his heart to God (who is great and mighty). And if they invite him to eat a bite or two, he does not permit his carnal soul to desire it.

It is not part of the ethics of disciples to perform numerous litanies, for the Sufis are occupied with clearing their minds of thoughts, remedying their character, and banishing heedlessness from their hearts, not with repetitive acts of piety. What is indispensable for them is performance of both religious duties and optional practices. But continuous recollection of God's names is more perfect for them than additional optional ritual prayers.

The chief possession of the disciple is forbearance with everyone, good nature, meeting whatever he encounters with satisfaction, patience during suffering and poverty, and giving up questioning and resistance, both in the dearth and the abundance that are one's lot. And whoever cannot endure that should go to the market, for whoever craves what the people crave should attain his desire the same way the people do it: by the labor of the hand and the sweat of the brow.

And if the disciple continually practices recollection and chooses seclusion, and if he experiences in his seclusion what no one has previously experienced, either sleeping or awake, or between waking and sleeping, such as hearing voices, or witnessing something out of the ordinary, he should have nothing to do with it. He does not dwell on it, nor should he look forward to attaining similar things. All such things are distractions from God (glory be to him). In such situations he should undoubtedly describe these experiences to his master so that his heart will be free of it.

It is necessary for the master to protect his disciple's secret, and to conceal his business from others, making little of it in itself. These are all tests, and dwelling upon them is a deception. Let the disciple beware of this and of paying attention to it, and let him aim his ambition beyond that.

Know that the most harmful thing for the disciple is to seek familiarity with these deceptive tests of God's approaches to him that he encounters in his conscience, and God's gift to him of saying, "I have distinguished you by this, and I have singled you out from your peers." If he decides to abandon this, he soon will be caught up by one of the real unveilings that will appear to him. But to explain all this by relying on books is impossible.

One of the duties of the disciple is that if he does not find someone to teach him in his own locality, he should travel to someone who is authorized to train disciples at that time. Then he should stay there, not moving from that master's threshold until given permission.

The disciple should not believe that the masters are infallible, and he should leave them and their spiritual states alone. He should think well of them and mind his own business with the help of God Most High. Religious knowledge is adequate for distinguishing between the praiseworthy and the defective.

If a disciple is afflicted by power, fame, association with boys, inclination toward women, or dreams of fame, and there is no master to guide him to an expedient solution that can free him from those problems, in such circumstances it is lawful for him to travel and depart from that place, since this condition disturbs him.

Part of the ethics of the disciple is that one's knowledge regarding this path should not outstrip his station. If one studies the lives of the Sufis, one should not try to understand their issues and their spiritual states without living experience and practice after reaching these spiritual realities. On this account the masters have said, "If the knower of God speaks of things of which he is ignorant, reports of spiritual stations are not the same as knowledge of them." One whose knowledge is superior to his spiritual stations is a scholar, not a mystic.

Another part of the ethics of disciples is that they do not

seek to put themselves forward or to have a student or a disciple of their own. If the disciple becomes a master before his human nature is pacified and before his faults are extinguished, he will be veiled from reality, and his allusions and teachings will benefit no one.

It is incumbent upon the disciple, if his path is service to the *faqir*s, that he should patiently bear their rough treatment of him. If he believes that he is expending his life in serving them, and then they do not praise him for anything, he should beg their forgiveness for his shortcomings. He should remain firm in attacking himself while staying in harmony with them. I heard the Imam Abu Bakr ibn Furak using a metaphor, "If you can't bear the blow, why become an anvil?"

The foulest quality in a disciple is to return to a desire that he has abandoned for the sake of God Most High. It is incumbent on the disciple to preserve his vows to God Most High, for if the vow is broken in the path of discipleship, it is similar to the outright rejection of religion among the followers of the external.

It is incumbent on the disciple to have little hope, for the Sufi is the son of the moment. And if he has a responsibility in the future, and he becomes aware of something other than the present, and he is hopeful of something that he is beginning, it will be of no use to him.

It is incumbent on the disciple to keep a distance from worldly people. Association with them is a dangerous poison. They make use of him while he is injured by them. God Most High said, "Do not obey one whose heart We have made forgetful of Our remembrance" (Q 18:28).

The master and imam Abu al-Qasim 'Abd al-Karim ibn Hawazin al-Qushayri (may God be pleased with him) said, This is our testament to the disciples. We ask generous God to grant them success, and not to place any evil upon us.

* * *

On Sainthood

The existence of spiritual masters is only made possible by sainthood, which is a state of nearness to God. Although it derives its authority from the prophets, and ultimately from God, sainthood is an ongoing reality in every age. The saint is literally the "friend" (*wali*) of God, and since the name "the Friend" is also one of the divine names, this is an attribute of divine origin. As with the master-disciple relationship, sainthood is one of the chief topics addressed by Sufi theorists. The author of this selection, 'Ala' al-Dawla Simnani (d. 1336), was a well-known member of the Kubrawi Sufi order in Central Asia. Like his predecessor, Najm al-Din Kubra (see chapter 3), he wrote a large number of works in Arabic and Persian, and he was extremely active in guiding and training students in the disciplines of meditation. This discussion of sainthood is a chapter from one of Simnani's comprehensive Persian treatises on the Sufi path. Simnani emphasizes the prophetic and divine origins of sainthood, and he stresses the need for repentance on the part of the spiritual aspirant as a pre-condition for purifying the soul enough even to perceive the character of a genuine saint. Only through divine assistance in the form of light can one reach the level of being able to perceive the reality of sainthood. Few have this ability except through hindsight. It is easy for anyone to go astray on the spiritual path, and therefore it is necessary to seek the aid of God and the saints themselves.

Repeating a prominent theme of early Sufism, Simnani gives a series of repeated warnings against attaching importance to miracles as a sign of sainthood. Instead, he maintains that inspired and understandable speech that is in accordance with the religious law is the surest sign of the character of the saint. Simnani then moves into a consideration of mystical psychology, based upon the complex notion of the seven subtle substances (*lata'if*) that make up the human psyche (see *The Shambhala Guide to Sufism*, p. 107). Since sainthood has relative degrees, Simnani points out that at each level the saint is likely to be persuaded that he has already attained the goal. This means that saints who have reached one level may denounce the experience of another level, because it does not accord with an experience that they regard as ultimate. In this situation, only the assistance of a saint of the highest order, such as one inspired by the Prophet's cousin and son-in-law 'Ali, can help one avoid the pitfall of premature spiritual claims.

Again asserting the prophetic origin of sainthood, Simnani takes the prophet Abraham as the model of how the saint should ascend through successive experiences to reach the goal of divine knowledge. Since the divine presence is in everything, Abraham at first believed that the Heavenly bodies were gods, and he worshiped them. When he realized that they rise and set, like transient experiences that come and go, he turned instead toward their Creator, who is beyond the changeable forms of creation.

from *The Clarification of Virtue for the People of Divine Knowledge*
'Ala' al-Dawla Simnani

Sainthood is illuminated by prophecy. My dear child, you who are a seeker of the water of life from the spring of sainthood! Know that sainthood is a capacity that derives from the mountain of the heart of the Prophet. But because of the clouds of desire and the vapors of passion that have arisen from one's physical body, that mountain gets blocked off from one's perspective, and one forgets that whole spiritual world. By frequent recollection, denial of thoughts, and abstaining from pleasant morsels and words, the veils produced by those smokes and vapors are lifted, and the heart of the saint is illuminated by the light of the Prophet. By that illumination he learns about the people and the saints of his country, and the good and bad that are found there.

Repentance as the means of purification. He exerts himself to strengthen his friends (the virtues) and weaken his enemies (the vices), and he pours the water of remorse upon the face of his spiritual state, which is blackened by betrayal of his friends and obedience to his enemies. That blackness can only be washed away with this water of remorse. To get that water to flow, one must obtain it from the water that is born from the salt mine of his eyelid. He thinks, "I can shed tears that resemble milk, or tears that are all turned to milk, and then the book of my deeds will be white." No man will find peace with God, God's people, or anything else, if that blackness remains on the face of his spiritual states, or a trace of that blackness is not turned to light, or the soul's understanding remains attached to food, speech, motion, and rest, and he does not totally reject that attachment to the body.

If one recognizes the necessity of following the eight conditions of retreat, as I have explained in the treatise *The Clear Victory*, every moment another revelation about one's true self descends from the divine presence.

> Your master is love; when you reach that place,
> He himself with the spirit's tongue speaks creation's
>　　word.

Sainthood as an attribute that derives from God. The purpose of this is for you to know the spiritual state of sainthood, for sainthood (*wilayat*) is a light that has emanated from a divine attribute. The divine name "the Friend" (*wali*) refers to this, for the divine word was recited by the tongue of the illiterate Prophet Muhammad (peace be upon him) in the expression, "God is the friend of those who have faith, bringing them from darkness into light" (Q 2:257). Muhammad (peace be upon him) recited this in the ears of his people. Those with the capacity to emanate that light seek its source. God Most High makes this light appear within the aspirant. God does this through a divine attribute, which is referred to by God's name "the Seeker" (*murid*).

The need for divine light. If the light of God's seeking does not emanate onto the heart, no heart can be capable of receiving the light of sainthood. That very light needs to know you. "God is the light of the Heavens and the earth" (Q 24:35). The Heavenly light is active and the earthly light is passive. God's saying "The earth shines with the light of its Lord" (Q 39:69) contains this reality. When both the Heavenly and earthly lights are linked together, "light upon light" (Q 24:35) is the result.

Divine light permits recognition of sainthood. My dear! To the degree that the disciple becomes more perfect, his heart (in which station the earth is dominant) becomes more receptive of the light of sainthood (which is dominated by Heaven). To the degree that the receptivity of his heart increases, the emanation of the light of sainthood becomes more powerful. The allusion of the Prophet Muhammad to this is well known: "My friends (the saints) are beneath my domes; no one knows them but me." It is certain that as long as the light of seeking God does not descend into the heart of the disciple, he cannot see the light of God's sainthood. "The domes of my friends" to which the Prophet alludes are nothing but the attributes of humanity that conceal the saints.

Few recognize the saints. One should gaze at the saints of God with the light of God, which you have within you, and not with the light of intellect and sensation, in order to be worthy of their sainthood. The carnal soul always gazes at human forms of the saints, from the sensory perspective, and the devil casts immature intellects into opposition. 'Abd Allah Ansari, the Master of Herat, has nicely said, "Disciples who recognize masters while they are living benefit from them, but deniers recognize them after their death, much to their sorrow."

No more than eighteen people recognized Bayazid (may God sanctify his secret) while he was alive, so that they could benefit from him. There were many others who exerted themselves to harm him. Today, when he has passed away, all the people have become disciples of his tomb, because they did not see his human form from the sensory perspective; they have only heard reports of his perfections.

It is easy to go astray without discipline. And if the carnal soul were not supposed to submit, and if one were not required to enter into the obligation of commandments and prohibitions that are contrary to one's nature, being a disciple would appear to be easy. When the devil ties up the helpless seeker's aspiration with doubt, so that he cannot arrive safe and sound from the source of the heart to the water of eternal life, from this deception the disciple simply turns another page, and he is satisfied that his path is that of perfection.

Seek the aid of God and the saints. My dear! Listen attentively to my advice, gaze upon the saints of God with respect, and do not let your intellect become the site of opposition, so that God may bring you up to the level that I intend for you (if God Most High wills).

My dear! If divine assistance is not the companion of the wayfarer, when will he ever reach the Ka'ba of union? If the light of God's seeking does not ignite the candle of guidance, how will the seeker see the beauty of his own sainthood?

Miracles distract from the love of God. My dear! On the path there are obstacles consisting of miracles both seen and reported. Beware, and do not be attracted to them; be certain that

> At every step there is a trap, my dear—
> Love is forbidden to weaklings, my dear.

That is, you are only a lover of your beloved and whatever else you are attracted to. God's saying "His gaze did not waver, nor was he aggressive" (Q 53:17, describing the Prophet Muhammad's ascension to the divine presence) is the story of the lover's sincerity.

> If you want me, cross out the whole world.
> Two beloveds don't fit nicely in one heart.

"God has not put two hearts inside any man" (Q 33:4).

> If you want me, tell my whole story.
> Fear me and get rid of the rest.
> I am beautiful, beautify my memory.
> Don't have a double heart with me—be one heart.

My dear! Visible gifts have become the portion of the fools among the people of the path, and sensational miracles have become the lot even of the wise among the people of this path. The Prophet (may God bless him and grant him peace) referred to both groups in his saying "Most of the people of Paradise are fools, but the Highest Heaven is for those who possess the inner heart." God said, "How can you know of the Highest Heaven?" My son! "It is a written book, witnessed only by those who are brought near" (Q 83:20–21). But the real lover should not even look at sensational miracles with the gaze of longing.

> Whatever befalls you on the path,
> Why call it faith or infidelity?
> When it is the beloved and your desires,
> How ugly or pretty can that picture be?

A veil is a veil, whether it is a rose or a thorn.

After union, wonders may take place. But when the Beloved comes to you, as the saying goes, "Every wild animal comes with its fur"; when everything comes to you (including miracles), take it. After this point, distinctions do take place among those who are brought near to God, by reason of God's saying "Above every knower is the truly knowing One" (Q 12:76).

By their speech you shall know them. My child! Know for certain that the fruit of the human tree is speech, and humanity is distinguished from the animals by language. You may consider someone as a quite noble tree, if God assists him by giving the gift of eloquent speech (the experience that your heart and soul understand), and if his intellect and learning do not thereby become the source of opposition. The distinction between the most excellent of human "trees," and the reason for preferring one to another, cannot be made except by what I have stated (i.e., the best of humanity are known through the fruits of their speech). The truthfulness of that claim is justly witnessed by the inimitability of the Qur'an, which was brought by the Seal of the Prophets, Muhammad. The saying of the perfect ones is "A man is concealed by his tongue until he talks." It is also said, "A man is known by his way of speaking, not by his clothing."

Mistakenly claiming union in the seven spiritual substances. Another error that befalls and deceives some who imagine themselves to have attained perfection on the path is that, having traveled the path and accomplished the task of virtue, they have come to the goal, but they have not given the gift of submission. Inevitably, when they reach the light of (1) *the subtle substance of the body*, they will raise the Pharaoh's cry of "I am your highest Lord" (Q 79:24). They do not know that they have only reached the first of the seven subtle substances; but the light of lordship has been placed in every subtle substance, and for that reason it is possible to learn from anything, even the most elementary of these levels. Likewise, when they reach the light of (2) *the subtle substance of the soul*, they raise to the stars Hallaj's shout of "I am the Truth."

There is a secret here that you should listen to. That is, one who reaches (3) *the subtle substance of the heart* finds that saying of Hallaj to be destructive and objectionable. Unlike Hallaj, he speaks in negation of himself and in affirmation of God, and he has firm faith eternally. He is in conflict with those who have reached the subtle substances of the body and the soul, for they speak in affirmation of themselves. Inevitably they are afflicted with the lowest levels of ignorance. Every wayfarer who reaches the lights of the subtle substances of (4) *the conscience,* (5) *the spirit,* (6) *the mystery,* and (7) *the reality,* who is not protected and says things like this, remains far from God and is imprisoned in the lowest levels of ignorance. Since I do not see much benefit from repeating this point, here I will fold up the carpet of explanation.

Help with visions from a saint inspired by 'Ali. There are also many errors that come in manifestations of form and light. But the wayfarer can find release from these difficult dangers, if he has come to the chamber of the perfect and perfecting guidance of sainthood, whose guidance is joined to the inspiration of the axis of the saints, 'Ali the chosen one (peace be upon him, the peace of God's Messenger and his friend), and the wayfarer gives the previously unrealized gift of submission.

Abraham as a model for finding the divine light beyond creation. My child! Every human being who has worshiped something and made that thing into an idol has done so because the light of divine worship was placed in all things, and all things are sustained by God. If they witness a minute portion of light or truth (without which nothing exists) in something, or if God Most High displays himself to them in a manifestation of form or light in the form of that minute portion of truth or light, and they ask themselves to interpret it, they fall into the danger of conceiving God in human terms and asserting two gods. Fire-worshipers, sun-worshipers, and idolaters actually reached the spirit by this path of misapprehension. But if the assistance of God Most High is one's companion, the wayfarer will be allowed to pass. He will resemble "the friend of the merciful one," Abraham (the prayers of the merciful one be upon him), who was gradually allowed to pass through these stages

when he was shown the Heavenly realm. Each time he was
shown the stars, the moon, or the sun, he said "This is my
Lord; this is my Lord; this is my Lord." But when he was
shown that all the Heavenly bodies set, he turned toward
"the Creator of the heavens and the earth" (Q 6:14). He
made this his prayer of the moment: "I have turned my face
to the One who created the Heavens and the earth, as a
worshiper of one God, for I am not one of the idolaters"
(Q 6:79).

Sometime the man of submission and faith will reach
the station of virtue, where he directly witnesses the One
whom he worships, without any defect of it setting. In the
station of meditation he also knows that God sees him, and
he realizes that God watches over him, by reason of God's
saying "God is the one who oversees His servants" (Q 3:15).

8

LIVES OF THE SAINTS

A S THE SUFI MOVEMENT unfolded, one of the greatest subjects of interest was the lives and characters of leading Sufis. The earliest collections of Sufi biographies focused primarily on their sayings, as a source of teaching, while later hagiographies increasingly stressed stories of virtuous actions and miraculous events. Some of these works were arranged by generations, going back to the earliest clearly recognizable generation of Sufi teachers in the ninth century. As time went on, biographies proliferated, and each region had its own special patron saints. This is not ordinary history. Reading these biographies, we find ourselves in a different world, where one encounters not only saintly men and women, but also representatives of the invisible spiritual hierarchy like the mysterious Substitutes, who could appear in the guise of an ordinary person. It is also taken for granted that the saints are living in their tombs, and that they can be approached by spiritual inspiration for their blessings and help.

Because of the vastness of this literature, it is not possible to represent the many different types of Sufi biographical writing here. As an example, however, I have chosen the biography of possibly the best-known Sufi, Jalal al-Din Rumi (d. 1273). He was born in the city of Balkh (present-day Afghanistan), but when he was a child his family journeyed west to avoid the onslaught of the Mongol armies. They eventually settled in the city of Konya (present-day Turkey), and there Jalal al-Din became first a theologian and later a mystic and poet, called simply "Mawlana" ("our Master") by his disciples. He is known by different names: the Afghans call him Balkhi, the Persians call him Mawlavi, the Turks call him Mevlana, and elsewhere he is known as Rumi (from the Arabic name of the eastern Roman Empire).

This particular biography is related by one of the outstanding Persian Sufi authors of the late medieval period, 'Abd al-Rahman Jami (d. 1492). A member of the Naqshbandi Sufi order, Jami was one of the leading literary figures in the Timurid court at Herat (present-day Afghanistan). *The Breezes of Intimacy from the Sacred Presences* is a collection of over six hundred biographies of Sufis, based on anthologies written several centuries earlier, and in it Jami attempts to give the fullest possible picture of Sufism. This biography of Rumi shows Jami's characteristic literary approach, based on specialized documents relating to Rumi's life. Although it includes miraculous stories and details of Rumi's way of life, the main stress is upon his teachings and his remarkably direct way of conveying spiritual truths. While much more could be said on the subject of Rumi, this account nevertheless provides a good example of the way that the great saints were perceived within the Sufi tradition.

The Life of Mawlana Jalal al-Din Rumi
JAMI

The birth of Mawlana Rumi took place in Balkh, on 6 Rabiʿ I, 604 [September 30, 1207]. It is said that, from the time he was five years old, the forms of the Merciful and the shapes of the Hidden—that is, the angels that record one's deeds, the pious jinn, and the chosen humans who are veiled in the domes of divine power—used to appear in his presence and take on a human shape.

The following report has been found in the handwriting of his father, the Master Baha' al-Din Walad: "Jalal al-Din Muhammad was six years old when one Friday, with several other children, he went up on the roof of our house. One of the children said to the others, 'Come on, let's jump from this roof to that other roof!' Jalal al-Din Muhammad said, 'This is the way that dogs, cats, and animals move. It would be a shame for a man to act like that. If you have the power in your soul, come and fly up to Heaven.' At once he disappeared from their sight. The children cried out, but after a minute he reappeared, with his complexion altered and his eyes transformed. He said, 'When I spoke to you, I saw that a group of people with green robes came to me because of your crying and shouting, and they brought me back down to this place.' " It is also said that, at that age, he used to fast one out of every three or four days.

They say that during the time when he and his family went to Mecca, he had the opportunity to meet the Master Farid al-Din ʿAttar, and the Master gave to him the *Book of Secrets*. He kept it with him always.

Mawlana Rumi said, "I am not this body that can be seen by the eyes of lovers, rather I am that longing and that consciousness that arises within disciples because of my words. God! God! When you find that breath, and when you taste that longing, carry it away with you, and give thanks, for I am that."

In the presence of Mawlana Rumi they said, "So and so says, 'My heart and soul are at your service.'" He said, "Silence! Has this lie come to be repeated by the people? Where has He found a heart and soul that is at the service of men?" Then he turned his face toward Chelebi Husam al-Din, saying, "God! God! One should sit knee to knee with the friends of God, for there is a tremendous influence in their proximity."

> One should not spend a moment far from Him,
> for distance gives rise to destruction.
> In every situation, be with Him,
> for compassion comes about from nearness.

The Master said, "The bird that flies up from earth, even though it does not reach Heaven, nevertheless is that much farther away from the trap, and so it escapes. Even so, if a person is a Sufi and does not reach the perfection of Sufism, nevertheless that person is to this extent distinguished from the masses and the businessman, escapes the sorrows of the world, and becomes free. 'Those who travel light are saved, while those who are weighed down are destroyed.'"

When he saw one of his companions in a mood of depression, he said, "All sadness comes from the heart's attachment to this world. You must know that every moment when you are free, you become a stranger to this world and yourself. You must know that every color you see, and every flavor you taste, is not really like you—you are going somewhere else. Then you will no longer be sad."

He said, "The free man is one who is not injured by injuring anyone, and the chivalrous one does not injure anyone who deserves to be injured."

The learned Siraj al-Din of Konya was the chief of charitable trusts, and a great man of his time, but he was not happy with Mawlana Rumi. In his presence people said that Mawlana Rumi had stated, "I am one with the seventy-three religious sects." Since he was an egotistical person, he wanted to punish the Master and shame him. He sent for one of his companions who was a great scholar, and said, "Ask the Master in front of the assembly whether he has said such a thing. If he admits it, insult him and punish him!" So that man came and questioned the Master, asking, "Have you said: 'I am one with the seventy-three religious sects'?" The Master said, "I have said it." That man opened his mouth and began to insult and curse. Mawlana Rumi laughed and said, "I am also one with what you have said." The man became embarrassed and retreated. Shaykh 'Ala' al-Dawla Simnani said, "This saying of his is wonderful."

Mawlana Rumi always used to ask his attendant, "Is there any food in our house today?" If the attendant said, "It's all right—there is nothing," the Master would become expansive and give thanks, saying, "Praise be to God, for our house today is like the house of the Messenger Muhammad (may God bless him and grant him peace)!" But if he said, "The kitchen is certainly ready," the Master would become disturbed and say, "The smell of Pharaoh is coming from this house."

They say that in his assembly, they never lit a candle, except on the rare occasion when there was no oil lamp. He would say, "The candle is for kings, but the oil lamp is for vagabonds."

Once in his assembly they told the story of Shaykh Awhad al-Din Kirmani (God have mercy on him), saying, "He was a man who loved physical beauty, but his affairs were Platonic, and he never did anything shameful." The Master said, "He should have just done it and moved on."

> Brother, this court has no end.
> There is a basis for everything you meet.

One day he said, "The sound of the lute is the squeaking of the door of Heaven, which we now can hear." A skeptic said, "We hear the same sound. How is it that we do not become as excited as the Master?" The Master said, "God forbid! What we hear is the sound of the door opening, and what he hears is the sound of the door closing."

The Master also said, "Someone came to a dervish retreat. The dervishes asked him, 'Why do you sit alone?' He replied, 'I sat alone for a moment, but you came to me from God to prevent that.'"

A group of people asked Mawlana Rumi to lead ritual prayers. The master Shaykh Sadr al-Din Qunawi was also present in that group. Mawlana Rumi said, "I am just one of the Substitutes, who sit down and get up wherever we happen to be. For a prayer leader, one should have a solid Sufi master." And he pointed to the master Shaykh Sadr al-

Din, indicating that he should lead prayers. The latter humbly yielded the position of prayer leader to Mawlana Rumi, replying in Arabic, "When you pray behind a leader who fears God, it is like praying behind a prophet."

Once the Master was listening to music. The question occurred to a dervish: What is poverty? In the middle of the music, the Master recited this Arabic quatrain:

> Poverty's the substance, all else is accident.
> Poverty's the cure, all else is disease.
> All the world is cheating and deception—
> Poverty's the secret and the purpose of this world.

He was asked, "Can a dervish sin?" He said, "If he eats without appetite, for to eat without appetite is a grave sin for dervishes."

They say that the revered lord Shams al-Din Tabrizi (may God sanctify his secret) said, "The sign of the successful disciple is that at first he cannot abide the company of strangers. But if he suddenly encounters a stranger, he sits with him just like a hypocrite in a mosque, a child in school, or a prisoner in jail."

In his final illness, Mawlana Rumi said to his companions, "Do not be sad on account of my departure. The light of Mansur Hallaj (God have mercy on him) after one hundred and fifty years illuminated the spirit of Shaykh Farid al-Din 'Attar (God have mercy on him) and became his master. Whatever state you are in, be with me and remember me, so that I may help you, in whatever garb I may be."

He also said, "I have only two attachments in this world: one to the body, and the other to you. When by the grace of God (glory be to Him) I become single and isolated, and I turn my face toward the world of solitude and isolation, that spiritual connection will also belong to you."

The revered Shaykh Sadr al-Din (may God sanctify his secret) came to visit him at this time. He said to the Master, "May God heal you with a swift remedy! May your spiritual degrees be lofty! I hope that you're well. The revered Master is the soul of humanity." Mawlana Rumi replied, "May God heal you next! A shirt finer than a hair lies between the lover and the Beloved. Don't you want the light to be joined to the light?

> "I was stripped of the body, he was stripped of
>   illusion—
> now I proudly stroll toward the final union."

The Shaykh wept with his companions, and the revered Master recited the poem that begins with this verse:

> What do you know of the King who sits within me?

Mawlana Rumi gave the following testament to his disciples in Arabic: "I counsel you to be aware of God both secretly and in public; to have little food, little sleep, and little speech; to shun crimes and acts of disobedience to God; to be persistent in fasting; to stand in meditation at length; to give up the desire for your own benefit; to bear oppression from all creatures; to avoid the company of the foolish crowd; to associate with the upright and the generous—for the best people are those who benefit others, and the best words are those that combine guidance with brevity. Praise belongs to God alone."

They asked him, "Who is worthy to succeed the Master?" He said, "Chelebi Husam al-Din." This question and answer was repeated three times. The fourth time they said, "What do you say about your son, Sultan Walad?" He replied, "He is a virtuous man, and there is no need for any testament from me concerning him." Chelebi Husam al-Din said, "Who should perform your funeral prayer?" He said, "Shaykh Sadr al-Din."

Mawlana Rumi then said, "Our friends pull us from one side, and Mawlana Shams al-Din Tabrizi calls from the other side. 'People! Answer the one who calls from God' (Q 46:31). Leaving is unavoidable."

He passed away (may God sanctify his secret) at sunset on 5 Jumadi II, 672 (December 17, 1273).

Shaykh Mu'ayyad al-Din Jandi was asked, "What did Shaykh Sadr al-Din say with respect to the revered Master?" He said, "By God! One day he was sitting with the elite lovers, such as Shams al-Din Ayki, Fakhr al-Din 'Iraqi, Sharaf al-Din Mawsili, and Shaykh Sa'id Farghani. Talk fell on the life and mystery of the Master. The revered Shaykh said, 'If Bayazid and Junayd were alive in this time, they would have humbly carried the saddle cloth of this true man, and they would have counted it a blessing for their souls. He is the cook at the feast of Muhammad's poverty. We are eager to be his assistants.' All of the companions present agreed and approved of this." After that, Shaykh Mu'ayyad said, "I too am a beggar in the court of this emperor." And he recited this Arabic verse:

> If the godhood had a form among us,
> it would be you, though I cannot breathe a word.

* * *

LIVES OF WOMEN SAINTS

ONE OF THE SUPERFICIAL truisms that passes for information about Islam in the media today is the commonly held notion that all Muslim women are oppressed. This view is so axiomatic that the vast majority of Americans assume that it is true, without anyone feeling the need to ask a real Muslim woman what her feelings are. The fact that the majority of Anglo-American converts to Islam are women suggests that the situation is a little more complex. Yet the impression consistently remains that Islam is a religion dominated by ruthless patriarchy. This impression is by no means without foundation; indeed, all the major religious traditions of the world have experienced similar forms of social organization through male-dominated political structures. At the same time, it is a fact that women have had an important spiritual role in the Islamic tradition, and this is almost completely unknown to most outsiders.

One way to approach the problem of gender role in Islam is to consider the dichotomy between the public and the private. In most Muslim societies, the public sphere has been reserved almost entirely for men, while the private realm has been the province of women. A modern Euro-American feminist critique would easily assume that this is simply unfair. Leaving aside the tendency to judge others by their actions and oneself by one's ideals, it must be pointed out that it is still possible to get some access to the spiritual lives of Muslim women. Yet there are limits. Jami concluded his Persian work *The Breezes of Intimacy* with an appendix entitled "On the Remembrance of the Women

Knowers of God Who Have Attained the Levels of the Men of God." In it he writes:

> The author of *The Meccan Openings*, Muhyi al-Din ibn al-'Arabi (God have mercy on him), in the seventy-third chapter, after mentioning some of the generations of the men of God, says, "Everything that we have said regarding these men, as men, includes women, though there is more reference to men. Someone was asked, 'How many "Substitutes" are there?' He replied, 'Forty souls.' He was asked, 'Why did you not say forty men?' He answered, 'Because there are women among them.'"
>
> The master Abu 'Abd al-Rahman al-Sulami, author of *Generations of the Masters*, compiled a memoir of the spiritual states of women devotees and knowers of God, and he clarified much in explanation of the spiritual states of many of them. The poet al-Mutanabbi has written a verse, alluding to the fact that "sun" is feminine and "moon" is masculine in Arabic:

> Were women as I have described,
> Women would be superior to men.
> Femininity is no defect in the sun,
> Nor should the moon be proud of masculinity.

The lost treatise of al-Sulami has been recently rediscovered, and it has been translated into English by Rkia Laroui Cornell in *Early Sufi Women* (Fons Vitae, 1999). This text permits us to see with a little more detail the ambiguity and sensitivity of the issue of gender in Sufi hagiography. This

problem was stated with particuliar force by one of the
women who figures in that anthology, 'A'isha bint Ahmad
of Merv: "Concealment is more appropriate for women
than unveiling, for women are not to be exposed." This is a
surprising answer that she gave to a question about the
mystical experience that the Sufis call unveiling. It is unex-
pected, because the text itself provides abundant evidence
of such spiritual experiences among women. But in a sense,
her answer illustrates one of the main problems confronting
anyone who seeks to understand Islam: how can we have
access to the feminine dimension of Islamic culture without trespassing in the private sphere?

On one level, the quotation suggests why male authors
included so few women in biographical works in general
and in biographies of Sufis in particular. That is, in most
cases, biographies of women (when given at all) are included as an appendix to the biographies of men that are
the "main" subject of the book. Certainly a tacit misogyny
was one attitude to be found in Sufi texts.

Still, on another level, the notion of concealment and
privacy for women may help explain both the relatively
small space granted to women in Sufi writings, and the
brevity and lack of personal detail in these biographies.
Where women do figure in Sufi biographies, one finds typical patterns of presentation that may well be explained by
predictable male-female dynamics. How many times has it
been said of an impressive woman, that she was, as it were,
a man in the form of a woman? This sort of negative com-
pliment seems to be the last resort of the male hagiographer
who is perplexed and bewildered (and struck with admira-

tion) by the spiritual power of a woman. In the translations that follow, a number of examples are given of biographical approaches to the spiritual lives of Muslim women, beginning with two accounts by Jami.

The first of these is the very famous early Sufi woman Rabi'a of Basra (d. 801), about whom much has been written—so much, indeed, that she sometimes serves as a kind of obligatory reference that permits one to forget to mention any other women afterward. The brief account given below emphasizes her amazing ability to cut to the essence of any spiritual problem, which she does typically by a kind of one-upmanship of the chief male Sufis of the day (see also the much longer notice of Rabi'a by 'Attar, translated by Paul Losensky, in Michael Sells, *Early Islamic Mysticism*, [Paulist Press, 1996]). This is followed by a down-to-earth account of Fidda (thirteenth century), a woman of Andalus, whose goat served as a medium to demonstrate how the heart has the power to transform outward circumstance.

Early Women Saints
JAMI

Rabi'a al-'Adawiyya

She belonged to the people of Basra. Sufyan Thawri (may God be pleased with him) posed certain questions to her, visited her, and requested her advice and prayers.

One day Sufyan came to her, extended his hand, and

said, "God! I ask you for security." Rabi'a wept. Sufyan asked, "What makes you weep?" She said, "You have brought me to weeping." Sufyan said, "How?" She replied, "Don't you know that security from the world means abandoning God, and that you are now defiled by this?"

Rabi'a said, "Everything has a fruit, and the fruit of divine knowledge is to come face to face with God Most High."

She also said, "I ask God's forgiveness for my lack of sincerity in asking His forgiveness."

Sufyan asked her, "What is the best thing by which the servant seeks nearness to God Most High?" She said, "That He knows that the servant loves nothing in this world or the next except God."

One day Sufyan said to her, "We have been saddened by God." She said, "Don't lie! If you were saddened, the world would not be enjoyable to you."

She also said, "My sorrow is not because I am sorrowful; my sorrow is because I am not sorrowful."

Fidda

Shaykh Abu al-Rabi' al-Malaqi said (God have mercy on him), "I heard of the spiritual state of a pious woman in a certain village. I had received an invitation to visit her to learn of the miracles for which she was famous. They called that woman Fidda. When I arrived in the village where that woman lived, they told me she had a goat that gave both milk and honey. I had bought a new jar, and I came before that woman and greeted her. Then I said, 'I'd like to see what they say your goat can do.' She brought the goat, we milked it and filled the jar, and then we drank it—it was milk with honey. I asked her the story of this. She said, 'We had a goat, though we are poor folk. On the day of the 'Id festival at the end of the fasting month of Ramadan, my husband, who was a pious man, said, "Today we will sacrifice this goat." I said, "Why? We are excused from making the sacrifice because of poverty, and God Most High knows how much we need this goat." By chance a guest happened to arrive that day, so I said to my husband, "We are obliged to honor the guest. Get up and kill it! But do it someplace where the children will not see, since killing it will make them cry." He took it outside to sacrifice it behind the wall. Suddenly I saw that the goat had jumped on the wall of the house and then came down into the house. I said, "Maybe that goat is running away from my husband." I went outside and saw that he was skinning the goat. I was amazed, and I told the tale to my husband. He said, "Perhaps God Most High has substituted a better one for it, so we may honor the guest." ' Then she said to me, 'My child, truly, what things has this goat done in the hearts of disciples! When their hearts are good and sweet, so is its milk, and if their hearts change, its milk also changes. May it make your hearts good!' "

Imam Yafi'i (God have mercy on him) says, "By 'disciples' that woman means herself and her husband, but she mentioned it in a general way for the sake of veiling and concealing, and to encourage disciples for the benefit of their hearts. This means when our hearts are good and sweet, so is that which is near us. Therefore, 'may it make your hearts good,' so that which is near to you may be good."

* * *

INDIAN WOMEN OF THE CHISHTI ORDER

IN INDIA TOO, one of the chief hagiographers saw fit to include a number of women in the appendix to a major collection of lives of the saints. This was *Reports of the Righteous on the Secrets of the Pious*, by 'Abd al-Haqq Muhaddith of Delhi, written in Persian in 1590. Both of the thirteenth-century women described below were related to important Sufis of the Chishti order. Although from reading these accounts, one has a sense of the powerful personalities of the women mentioned here, nevertheless they are so obscured that they can only be mentioned indirectly. In both these cases, it is their reputation after death, even in the mere vicinity of their tombs, that indicates the halo of sanctity with which they were surrounded.

from *Reports of the Righteous on the Secrets of the Pious*
'ABD AL-HAQQ MUHADDITH DIHLAWI

Bibi Sara

She was the mother of Shaykh Nizam al-Din Abu al-Mu'ayyad, a very great saint, from the first generations. It is said that once there was a drought, and all the people prayed, but no rain came. Shaykh Nizam al-Din Abu al-Mu'ayyad took a thread from the skirt of his mother and said, "Lord, by the holiness of the one to whom this weak skirt-thread belongs, who has never been seen by a forbidden eye, send rain!" As soon as the master said these words, God sent rain. Her tomb is by the side of the old prayer ground, opposite the tomb of Khwaja Qutb, south of Delhi (God have mercy on her).

Bibi Fatima Sam

She is one of the pious and humble women devotees of the age. She is frequently mentioned in the discourses of Shaykh Nizam al-Din Awliya' and his disciples. They say that the emperor of the masters, Shaykh Nizam al-Din Awliya', frequently meditated in the shrine of Fatima Sam. Shaykh Farid al-Din Ganj-i Shakar said, "Fatima Sam is a man sent in the form of woman."

Shaykh Nizam al-Din said, "When the lion has come out of the forest, nobody asks if it is male or female; the children of Adam must obey and show respect, whether it is male or female. Now, in the stories of Fatima Sam there has been much said regarding her extreme piety and old age. I have seen her. She was a great woman. She was the adopted sister of Shaykh Farid al-Din and Shaykh Najib al-Din Mutawwakil. She recited verses on every subject. I have heard these two lines from her:

> You may seek love, and you may seek the soul.
> Seek them both, but it won't be easy.

I have heard from Bibi Fatima Sam that she said, 'The saints will cast away both worldly and religious blessings to give a piece of bread or a drink of water to someone in need. This state is something one cannot obtain by one hundred thousand fasts and prayers.' "

In the discourses of Mir Sayyid Gisu Daraz, it is written that one day in the assembly of Shaykh Nasir al-Din Mahmud, talk fell upon the virtues of Bibi Fatima Sam. He said, "Bibi Fatima Sam after her death told someone, 'One day by appointment I went to the revered Lord of Power (i.e., God). I passed by the round of angels, and suddenly an angel said, "Who are you? Why should you be proceeding so carelessly?" I replied, "I have sworn an oath; I am just sitting here until the Most High Lord of Power summons me; I will go no further." An hour passed. Bibi Khadija and Bibi Fatima Zahra, the wife and the daughter of the Prophet Muhammad (may God be pleased with them), came, and I fell at their feet. They said to me, "Fatima Sam, who is there like you today? For God Most High has sent us in search of you." I said, "I am your slave; what honor could be higher than for you to come in search of me? But I have sworn an oath." Then the decree came from God: "Fatima Sam speaks rightly. You both must depart from here and leave her alone." Then I heard God call, "Come to Me, to Me." I moved from that place. To God I said, "Lord, in Your presence there are such mannerless ones that Your visitors will not recognize You." ' She spoke these words, and sighed, from the midst of her tomb."

In *The Best of Assemblies,* the discourses of Shaykh Nasir al-Din Mahmud Chiragh-i Dihli, he says, "One day, Maw-

lana Husam al-Din came into the presence of Shaykh
Nizam al-Din (may God sanctify their secrets). He said,
'Mawlana Husam al-Din, today we saw one of the Substitutes.' He asked, 'Where did you see him?' He said, 'I was
making pilgrimage to the tomb of Bibi Sam; it is near the
enclosure of a pool. A man appeared carrying cucumbers
on his head, which he brought down to the edge of the
pool. He stored the cucumbers away and performed ablutions in such a way that I was astonished. When he finished
his ablutions, he performed two cycles of ritual prayer with
perfect equanimity. I was astonished from the experience
of seeing his prayer. Then he went in the water and washed
his basket three times. Then, one by one, he washed the
cucumbers, offered prayers to the Prophet, and put them
in the basket, until he had washed all the cucumbers in
this fashion. Then he picked up the basket and three times
put it down in the pool. He picked it up again, and set
it on the edge so that the water trickled out. From utter
astonishment, I arose. There was a silver coin in my turban,
which I took out and offered to him. I said, "Master, accept
this." He said, "Shaykh, excuse me." I said, "Master, for a
couple of coppers you wash your cucumbers repeatedly and
take such pains; God Most High now sends you a silver
coin as alms. Why won't you take it?" Again he said, "Excuse me." I said, "Give us the explanation; why won't you
take it?" He said, "Sit down, so I can tell you." That man
and I both sat down. He began:

   " ' "My father used to do the same job. I was small when
my father passed away. My mother taught me enough rules
of worship that I knew how to pray five times a day. After
that, when the hour of her passing took place, she called
me near and said, 'We have tied up something with a knot;

get it out and bring it.' I put my hand on that thing, and there was a knot on it. I put it before my mother. She opened it up, and did something particular. She said, 'This is the way to prepare the burial shroud, to wash the corpse, and to perform the burial in the tomb.' She gave me about twenty dirhams and said, 'This is the fortune of your whole life. When your father went into the gardens, he picked cucumbers and vegetables and sold them. Thus he spent his life. You also pick cucumbers and vegetables and sell them. Don't support yourself in any way but this.' "

" 'When the man finished this tale, I realized that he was one of the Substitutes. He accepts nothing from anyone except under duress (God have mercy on him and on all the pious).' "

In *Lives of the Saints* by Mir Khwurd, he says that Bibi Fatima Sam is buried in the outskirts of Indrapat township. Her shrine has become the place where people go for help with their needs. The writer of these lines observes that her tomb today is near the Nakhas Gate of Delhi, but it has fallen into ruin, so that no one knows it except if God wills. The place that the vulgar call "Bibi Sham," or which some common people call "the fasting (*sa'im*) Bibi"—in both cases erroneously—is correctly named after Bibi Fatima Sam (God have mercy on her).

* * *

Baghdadian Women of the Rifaʻi Order

In contrast, one can see much greater detail in the following biographies of two women from the family of an important saint of Baghdad, the wife and daughter of Shaykh Ahmad al-Rifaʻi (d. 1178), founder of the Rifaʻi Sufi order. The wife is named after the famous early woman saint Rabiʻa al-ʻAdawiyya of Basra, while the daughter is named after a wife of the Prophet Muhammad, Zaynab. Their biographer, Abu Muhammad al-Witri (d. 1512), unambiguously describes them as scholars and as spiritual masters superior to men. His accounts draw upon literary documents of an earlier period, and so it appears that the reputation of these saintly women was well established in the Sufi literature of the day. Despite their fame, it is clear that they felt they had different roles from the saintly men in their family.

from *The Garden of the Guardians and the Extract of the Deeds of the Upright*
ABU MUHAMMAD AL-WITRI (D. 1512)

Rabiʻa bint Abi Bakr

Among the saints is the woman master (*shaykha*), the long-lived knower of God, Rabiʻa [d. 1216], the daughter of the illustrious shaykh Abu Bakr al-Najari al-Wasiti. It is said in *The Clarification* that the noble lady, the perfect knower of God, the wife of Sayyid Ahmad, the mother of Sayyid Salih, the lady of the *faqir*s, Rabiʻa, was sound of heart and pure of mind. She experienced divine attractions and constant sorrow. No one could blame her for anything

before God. She had a beautiful life and admirable qualities. Sayyid Ahmad called her "the lady of the *faqir*s," and
he also nicknamed her "the mother of the *faqir*s." He said,
"Your service to the *faqir*s is indispensable." Once she wept
before Sayyid Ahmad and said, "What will become of me
after you are gone? I will be alone and the gate of happiness
and delight will be locked in my face." He said (may God
be pleased with him), "The people of the kingdom will
serve you, and your word will be heard. Your blessings will
be enduring." The family of Sayyid Ahmad was bound by
that promise for the rest of her life. She used to stop by the
tomb of her husband and speak with him, listening to his
reply. She did not honor anyone as a saint after the death
of her husband except if she knew it from personal experience. She asked her Lord if the succession of Sayyid Muhammad was confirmed. Regarding her death, she passed
away on Friday, the tenth of the month of Shawwal, 613 in
the Muslim era [February 1, 1216]. She was buried in the
blessed dome of her husband's tomb, in Baghdad.

Zaynab bint al-Rifaʿi

It is said in *The Clarification* that among the saints was
the patient, humble lady, the one who recollected God, the
perfect woman saint, the pure knower of God, the pious
God-fearing one, the hopeful luminous one, the one who
took precedence over saintly men, through her lofty qualities and her illustrious spiritual states, the mistress of sublime degrees, the mother of men, my lady Zaynab [d.
1232]—I mean the daughter of the supreme savior, Imam

al-Rifa'i (may God be pleased with her and him, and may He illuminate her tomb and whiten her page with His excellence). She wore rough clothing and gave up fine food and drink. She wore out her veil, and inclined to the service of God, the generous King. She was content with simplicity despite her power, and she served the needs of her father and followed his example. Her spiritual path was humility and contrition, and her habit was peace and poverty. Sayyid Ahmad used to say (may God be pleased with him), "It was as though she had been created a man, and the people thought she was created a woman."

Sayyid 'Umar al-Faruthi said, "One day I was with Sayyid Ahmad, and he revealed to me many of his secrets. Then he took me by the hand and took me into his house, to his wife Rabi'a [described in the previous biography]. He said, 'Greet her, and ask her to pray for you.' Then came his daughter, my lady Zaynab, and he kissed her head. Then he said to me, "Umar! Greet her, serve her, and ask her to pray for you and your offspring.' I did that, but then I said to myself, 'It would have been more appropriate if he had told me instead to serve and honor her mother, my lady Rabi'a, since she is the elder.' Perceiving my thought, Sayyid Ahmad turned to me (may God sanctify his glorious secret) and said to me, ''Umar! God promised me that He would give life to the tradition through the lady Zaynab, and that He would make the lands flourish through her.' My lady Zaynab said to him, 'My lord, you are alive, and so is your son Sayyid Salih; God has put me here as your sacrifice, and he will give life to the tradition through you.' Sayyid Ahmad said, 'Rather, by you.' So she said, 'My lord, shall I sit and speak to the people, and hold assemblies with them?' And he said to her, 'Zaynab, no; rather, your offspring will endure until Resurrection Day.' " However, the author of *The Remedy* relates this story in his book without the same sequence.

Maryam, the daughter of Shaykh Yaʻqub, said, "My lady Zaynab spoke to me of life and death: 'We work a little and seek rest at length. The goal is far and the path is long, the body is weak and the supplies few, but we cannot avoid this journey. If we take it before it takes us, and if we welcome it before it welcomes us, it will be better for us.' "

Al-Zabarjadi said, "She learned the Qur'an, studied Islamic law, and heard the sayings of the Prophet from her uncle, Shaykh Abu al-Badr al-Ansari al-Wasiti. Her sons, all notable leaders, studied with her, and one who heard the sayings of the Prophet from her was the great Shaykh ʻUmar Abu al-Faraj al-Faruthi al-Kazaruni. She was very powerful and had a lofty station."

An army of locusts attacked the fields of the people of Wasit and Umm ʻUbayda, and the people turned to her for help. She donned a veil and went up on the roof and said, "God! The people are driven by their good opinion of me, and You are the one who has put that into their hearts. I am not worthy to ask You this, because of my sins and my failures, but You are too generous to reject the wretched, Most Merciful One!" Then the locusts seemed to be held back by reins, as though they were camels led by herdsmen, so that not a single locust remained in the lands of Wasit. This lioness is descended from that lion, Sayyid Ahmad al-Rifaʻi.

She died in the year 630 (1232) at Umm ʻUbayda, and

she is buried in the blessed Ahmadi shrine (may God be pleased with her).

* * *

A Sufi Princess, Jahanara

ALTHOUGH RELATIVELY few non-elite Muslim women left well-attested literary legacies, among upper-class women there was much freer access to education as well as the possibility of acting as a patron for religious and cultural activities. Jahanara (1614–1681) was a daughter of the Mughal emperor Shahjahan, builder of the Taj Mahal. Like her brother Dara Shikuh (pictured on the front cover), she was drawn to Sufism, and like him she is the author of biographical works on contemporary and historical Sufi saints. She was also responsible for the creation of a number of Mughal gardens and other architectural projects. She wrote a biography of her Sufi teacher Mulla Shah as well as an account of the famous Indian saint of the Chishti order, Mu'in al-Din Chishti (d. 1236). It is from the latter text that the following autobiographical remarks derive. She is buried in a small white marble tomb, open to the elements and devoid of any dome, outside the shrine of the Chishti saint Nizam al-Din Awliya' in Delhi. The inscription reads as follows:

He is the Living, the Sustaining.
Let no one cover my grave except with greenery,
For this very grass suffices as a tomb cover for the poor.
The annihilated *faqir* Lady Jahanara,
Disciple of the Lords of Chisht,

Daughter of Shahjahan the Warrior
(may God illuminate his proof).

Jahanara's biography of the Indian founder of the Chishti
Sufi order, though compiled from existing works on Sufi
saints, is highly regarded for its judgment and literary quality. The conclusion and an appendix, which describes the
author's pilgrimage to Mu'in al-Din's tomb at Ajmer in 1643,
convey the author's personal engagement with Sufi practice. There she uses the word *faqira*—the feminine form of
faqir—to signify her own spiritual vocation as a Sufi
woman. She clearly regarded Mu'in al-Din Chishti as the
supreme Sufi saint of India and as the master who initiated
her, over four centuries after his death (initiation is referred
to by the expression "taking the hand," which is the ritual
gesture that seals this relationship). At the same time she
also remembers her living Sufi master, Mulla Shah. Her
pilgrimage was timed to coincide with the death anniver-
sary of the saint, and at his tomb she performed the customary rituals that are still carried out at Sufi shrines
around the world, including the recitation of prayers and
sections of the Qur'an, with the dedication of their benefit
to the inhabitants of the tomb. As she indicates, the
mosque where she prayed in Ajmer had been recently re-
constructed by her father Shahjahan; like many other rul-
ers, the Mughals erected extensive monuments at the
tombs of Sufi saints, as a sign of their devotion and in hope
of saintly assistance. Although this passage offers the re-
flections of a disciple rather than a master, it affords an
interesting glimpse into the practice of Sufi piety among
the royal class.

from *The Confidant of Spirits*

JAHANARA

Know that, after the performance of religious duties, re-
quirements, and the recitation of the holy Qur'an, this weak
woman who hopes for salvation regards no action as nobler
than the remembrance of the spiritual states and stations
of the revered saints (may God sanctify their spirits).
Therefore, I have spent a portion of my time in reading
books and treatises that contain the felicitous accounts of
the great ones of religion and the mighty ones of certainty.
This *faqira* had such perfect sincerity and devotion that I
wrote a summary of the career of the revered master who
took my hand in discipleship, as well as the chief succes-
sors of that revered one (may God inspire their spirits).

Praise and favor be to God, for by the assistance of God
the Knower, the Powerful, and with the helping grace of
the revered master who took my hand, I attained this desire
of mine, and this treatise *The Confidant of Spirits* was ed-
ited and put on the robe of completion on the 27th of the
blessed month of Ramadan, 1049 (January 21, 1640).

The lives of these great ones, who are the close ones of
the court of Eternity, having been extracted with great care
from well-known books and treatises, have been committed
to writing. In the belief of this weak woman, whatever is
affirmed in this text is completely correct. I hope that readers will have the full blessing and benefit of it. . . .

After praising the one God—and He is all eternal, great
is His majesty—and following the adoration of His messen-

ger Muhammad the chosen one (may God bless him and grant him peace)—this lowly *faqira* Jahanara, with the aid of fortune and ascendant victory, went from the capital Agra in the company of my great father toward the pure region of incomparable Ajmer. From the 17th of Sha'ban 1053 to Friday the 7th of the blessed month of Ramadan [October 31 to November 19, 1643], when I entered the building on the shore of the Anasagar tank, I was committed to this idea, that every day in every station I would perform two cycles of optional prayer. Then, having recited the Book of ys (Q 36) and the Opening (Q 1) with perfect sincerity and devotion, I bestowed the reward for that on the generous, pure, illuminated spirit of the revered master Lord Mu'in al-Din Chishti (may God be pleased with him).

For the several days when I stopped in the above mentioned buildings, from extreme courtesy I did not sleep on a leopard skin that night, I did not extend my feet in the direction of the blessed sanctuary of the revered saving master, and I did not turn my back toward him. I passed the days beneath the trees.

By the blessing of that revered one, and the gracious influence of this Heavenly land, I experienced concentration and mystical experiences. One night I performed a wonderful birthday and lamp festival for the saint. I did not stint in adorning and serving the blessed sanctuary with what I had and will have, nor will I ever do so.

Praise and favor be to God, and a hundred million thanks, for on Thursday, the fourth of the blessed month of Ramadan, I attained the happiness of pilgrimage to the illuminated and perfumed tomb of the revered saving master (may God be pleased with him). With an hour of daylight remaining, I went to the holy sanctuary and rubbed my pale face on the dust of that threshold. From the doorway to the blessed tomb I went barefoot, kissing the ground. Having entered the dome, I went around the light-filled tomb of my master seven times, sweeping it with my eyelashes, and making the sweet-smelling dust of that place the mascara of my eyes.

At that moment, a marvelous spiritual state and mystical experience befell this annihilated one, which cannot rightly be written. From extreme longing I became astonished, and I do not know what I said or did.

Finally with my own hand I put the highest quality of attar on the perfumed tomb of that revered one, and having taken off the rose scarf that I had on my head, I placed it on top of the blessed tomb. Having gone to the marble mosque erected by the great and God-knowing father of this lowly woman, I performed ritual prayer, and then, sitting in the blessed dome, I recited the Book of ys (Q 36) and the Opening (Q 1) for the generous spirit of the master. I was in that place until sunset prayer, and I lit a candle to the spirit of that revered one. I broke my fast with spring water. It was a marvelous night I saw there, which was better than the dawn.

If the sincerity, love, and spiritual concentration of this annihilated one demanded that I should not go back home after having gone all the way to that blessed and gracious place, the corner of security—what can be done?

> The Beloved has placed a noose on my neck,
> And He pulls me wherever He wishes.

If I had the choice, I would always have stayed in the sanctuary of that revered one, which is the marvelous corner of security—and I am a lover of the corner of security. I would also have had the honor and happiness of walking around it continuously.

Unwillingly, weeping and with burning heart, with a hundred thousand cries, I was excused from the court of that revered one and came home. All night long a wonderful restlessness was in me. That Friday morning, my great father ordered that we head toward Agra.

I have presented this elegant, noble, and sublime book, which this lowly woman compiled from well known books and treatises according to their value, having collected it and entitled it *The Confidant of Spirits*, as the perfect and felicitous life of that revered saving master (may God be pleased with him), so that it may always be in the illuminated and blessed sanctuary.

It is hoped that, from the complete grace and great generosity of that revered one, he will confer special acceptance on this treatise by this least of his devoted disciples, that he will be happy, and that he will turn his attention upon this woman disciple.

> Our Mu'in al-Din is annihilated in God,
> And after that he subsists in the absolute essence.

This lowly one is a *faqira* who is in the reality of realities, by the blessing of the saving master, the revered lord Mu'in al-Din Chishti, and from the external and internal attention of the real master, the revered Mulla Shah (may God lengthen his shadow and preserve him). Fictitious existence has gone, and that endless existence remains by itself.

NOTES ON SOURCES

1. MYSTICAL UNDERSTANDING OF THE QUR'AN

"The Book of the Elect: On Understanding and Following the Book of God," chaps. 38–41 from *The Book of Flashes* by Sarraj (d. 988): Abū Nasr ʿAbdallah B. ʿAlī al-Sarrāj al-Tūsī, *The Kitāb al-Lumaʿ fī ʾl-Tasawwuf*, ed. Reynold Alleyne Nicholson, "E. J. W. Gibb Memorial" Series, vol. 22 (London, 1914; reprint ed., London: Luzac & Company Ltd., 1963), pp. 72–79 (Arabic). I have also consulted the German translation by Richard Gramlich, *Schlaglichter über das Sufitum*, Freiburger Islamstudien, 13 (Stuttgart: Franz Steiner Verlag, 1990), pp. 131–39; and the Urdu translation by Sayyid Asrar Bukhari, *Kitab al-Lumaʿ* (Lahore: Islamic Book Foundation, 1405/1984), pp. 119–40.

2. THE CHARACTER OF THE PROPHET MUHAMMAD

THE PROPHET MUHAMMAD AS PRIMORDIAL LIGHT: *The TS of the Lamp*, by Hallaj (d. 922): "Hallağ, *Kitab al-Tawasin*," ed. Paul Nwyia, *Mélanges de l'Université Saint-Joseph*, 47 (Beirut: Imprimerie Catholique, 1972), pp. 191–94 (Arabic). This supersedes the edition and French translation of this text by Louis Massignon, which is faulty in a number of respects. The English version of the *Kitab al-Tawasin* by ʿAʾisha ʿAbd al-Rahman al-Tarjumana is tendentious and unreliable.

THE PROPHET MUHAMMAD AS MORAL EXEMPLAR: "The Book of the Example and Imitation of the Messenger of God," chaps. 47–50, from *The Book of Flashes*, by Sarraj: *The Kitáb al-Lumaʿ*, pp. 93–104 (Arabic); German translation by Gramlich, pp. 157–70; Urdu translation by Bukhari, pp. 157–77.

3. Spiritual Practice

CONDITIONS OF THE SPIRITUAL PATH, second to fifth conditions from *The Bewildered Traveler*, by Najm al-Din Kubra (d. 1220): Najm al-Din Kubra, *al-Sayir al-hayir*, ed. Mas'ud Qasimi (Tehran: Kitabfurushi Zavvar, 1361/1983), pp. 22–37 (Persian).

MEDITATIONS OF THE SHATTARI ORDER: *The Treatise on Meditation* and *The Treatise on the Intermediate State*, by Shah 'Isa Jund Allah (d. 1622): *Risala-i muraqaba* and *Risala-i barzakh*, in MS Persian JF 73, Maulana Azad Library, Aligarh Muslim University, Aligarh (Persian).

ASCENSION THROUGH THE PLANETARY SPHERES: *The Nine Lodges,* from *The Treasury of Incantations* by Isma'il ibn Mahmud Sindhi Shattari: *Makhzan-i da'vat*, MS Curzon Persian 437, Asiatic Society, Calcutta (Persian), fols. 111a–114a.

PRACTICES OF THE ORDERS, from *The Clear Fountain*, by Muhammad al-Sanusi (d. 1853): Muhammad ibn 'Ali Sanusi, *Al-Silsabil al-ma'in fil-tara'iq al-arba'in* (Cairo: n.p., 1989, pp. 88–90, 93–94 (Arabic).

4. Divine and Human Love

"On the Courtesy of the Lover and Beloved," from *The Jasmine of the Lovers* by Ruzbihan Baqli (d. 1209): Ruzbihan Baqli, *'Abhar al-'ashiqin*, ed. Henry Corbin and Muhammad Mu'in, Bibliothéque Iranienne, 8 (Tehran: Institut Français d'Iranologie de Téhéran, 1958; reprint ed., Tehran: Intisharat-i Manuchihri, 1365/1981), pp. 4–12 (Persian), with reference to the French translation and notes on pp. 112–125.

5. Listening to Music

"On Listening to Music," from *The Treatise on Holiness*: Ruzbihan Baqli Shirazi, *Risalat al-quds wa ghalatat al-salikin*, ed. Javad Nurbakhsh (Tehran: Khaniqah-i Ni'mat Allahi, 1351/1973), pp. 50–54 (Persian); French translation by Jean During, *Musique et extase. L'audition mystique dans la tradition soufie* (Paris: Albin Michel. 1988), pp. 210–16.

THE PRACTICES OF LISTENING TO MUSIC: Mushtaq Ilahi Faruqi, *Naghmat-i sama'* (Karachi: Educational Press, 1392/1972), pp. 240–43, 247–53 (Urdu).

6. ETHICAL PRACTICE

The Errors of Wayfarers, by Ruzbihan Baqli: Ruzbihan Baqli Shirazi, *Risalat al-quds wa ghalatat al-salikin*, pp. 81–102 (Persian).

7. MASTERY AND DISCIPLESHIP

"The Testament to Disciples" from *The Epistle* of al-Qushayri: Abu al-Qasim 'Abd al-Karim al-Qushayri, *al-Risala al-Qushayriyya*, ed. 'Abd al-Halim Mahmud and Mahmud ibn al-Sharif (Cairo: Dar al-Kutub al-Haditha, 1974), pp. 731–51 (selections) (Arabic).

ON SAINTHOOD, from *The Clarification of Virtue for the People of Divine Knowledge* by 'Ala' al-Dawla Simnani (d. 1336): *Bayan al-ihsan li-ahl al-'irfan*, in 'Ala' al-Dawla Simnani, *Musannafat-i Farsi [Persian Writings]*, ed. Najib Mayil Haravi (Tehran: Shirkat-i Intisharat-i 'Ilmi va Farhangi, 1369/1991), pp. 237–42 (Persian).

8. LIVES OF THE SAINTS

The Life of Mawlana Jalal al-Din Rumi: 'Abd al-Rahman Jami (d. 1492), *Nafahat al-uns min hadarat al-quds [The Breezes of Intimacy from the Sacred Presences]*, ed. Mahmud 'Abidi (Tehran: Intisharat-i Ittila'at, 1370/1992), pp. 461–65 (Persian).

LIVES OF WOMEN SAINTS: Early Women Saints (Rabi'a al-'Adawiyya, Fidda): Jami, *Nafahat*, pp. 613–14, 621–22 (Persian).

INDIAN WOMEN OF THE CHISHTI ORDER (Bibi Sara, Bibi Fatima Sam): 'Abd al-Haqq Muhaddith Dihlawi al-Bukhari, *Akhbar al-akhyar fi asrar al-abrar* [Reports of the Righteous on the Secrets of the Pious], ed. Muhammad 'Abd al-Ahad (Delhi: Matba'-i Mujtaba'i, 1332/1913–1914), pp. 294–96 (Persian).

BAGHDADIAN WOMEN OF THE RIFA'I ORDER (Rabi'a bint Abi Bakr, Zaynab bint al-Rifa'i): Ahmad ibn Muhammad al-Witri (d. 1512), *Rawdat al-nazirin wa khulasat manaqib al-salihin* [Garden of the Guardians and Extract of the Deeds of the Upright] (Cairo: al-Matba'a al-Khayriyya, 1306/1888), pp. 117–19 (Arabic).

A SUFI PRINCESS, JAHANARA (1614–1681), *Mu'nis al-arwah* [The Confidant of Spirits], in Qamar Jahan Begam, *Princess Jahan Ara Begam, Her Life and Works* (Karachi: S. M. Hamid 'Ali, 1991), pp. 117–23 of Persian text.

INDEX OF QUR'ANIC PASSAGES
AND PROPHETIC SAYINGS

QUR'ANIC PASSAGES

Here are listed all the passages from the Qur'an quoted in *Teachings of Sufism*, listed in numerical order according to book (*sura*) and verse (*aya*); on average, the sacred Book appears once on nearly every page. Not all of the quotations comprise a full verse, and whenever necessary a full translation has been supplied to provide a more understandable context.

Prophetic Sayings

Below are listed the sayings of the Prophet Muhammad that are quoted in the text. Although not all of them are to be found in the most authoritative collections of *hadith*, many of these are very well known, especially in Sufi circles. They are considered to be the words of Muhammad, except in the case of the Divine Sayings (*hadith qudsi*), the extra-Qur'anic revelations that Muhammad transmitted from God.

Printed in the United States
by Baker & Taylor Publisher Services